"I had the privilege of attending Ray Leonardini's centering prayer gathering at Folsom State Prison. I was touched by the depth of the practice shared in the group, and the peace those men have found in their lives. The dear men that I met that evening are testimony to this deep and heartfelt practice. As a tool for spiritual transformation, it clearly works! I hope you will give this practice a try. I wish that kind of peace for each of you."
—**Sita Lozoff**, Human Kindness Foundation

"**Finding God Within** is an amazingly concise yet profound collection of teachings that are both ancient and novel. The book teaches the ancient contemplative prayer practice that Father Thomas Keating has renewed with his centering prayer movement. But the book is novel as well. Its many striking features include powerful quotes from prisoners who are following this spiritual practice. This book offers all of us, no matter where we are serving time, a way to open our hearts to the God who heals, the God within."
—**Scott Wood**, Clinical Professor, Director of the Center for Restorative Justice, Loyola Law School of Los Angeles

ALSO BY RAY LEONARDINI

Going Inside

*Learning to Teach Contemplative Prayer
to the Imprisoned*

Finding God Within

Contemplative Prayer for Prisoners

RAY LEONARDINI

Prison Contemplative Fellowship

Lantern Books ● New York
A Division of Booklight Inc.

2016
Lantern Books
128 Second Place
Brooklyn, NY 11231
www.lanternbooks.com

For additional copies, free to prisoners, please write to: Prison Contemplative Fellowship, P.O. Box 1086, Folsom, CA 95763-1086, USPCF.org, email: office@USPCF.org.

This book is an updated and newly edited Lantern edition of the same title, published privately, in two editions, by the author.

Printed in the United States of America

Library of Congress Cataloging-in-Publication Data

Names: Leonardini, Ray, author.
Title: Finding God within : contemplative prayer for prisoners / Ray Leonardini.
Description: New York City : Lantern Books, 2016.
Identifiers: LCCN 2016032930 | ISBN 9781590565513 (pbk.)
Subjects: LCSH: Contemplation. | Prayer—Christianity. | Prisoners—Religious life.
Classification: LCC BV5091.C7 L45 2016 | DDC 248.3/4086927—dc23
LC record available at https://lccn.loc.gov/2016032930

All biblical quotations are from the New American Standard Bible unless otherwise indicated.

Prison Contemplative Fellowship is a community of prisoners, former prisoners, their families, chaplains, and volunteers who practice a form of Christian silent prayer called centering prayer. It is a fellowship that recognizes our individuality and celebrates our unique relationship with the Divine.

The symbol of the Cross, adapted for prisoners, points to the key to our freedom. We acknowledge that it is through the mysterious transformation of our suffering in centering prayer that brings the vital change we deeply desire.

*We are all prisoners, in one form or another,
and some of us are behind bars.*

Be still and know that I am God.—**Psalm 46:10**

Contents

Preface to the Third Edition xiii

Introduction. *Contemplative Prayer:*
A Path to Personal Transformation 1

Part 1. *Contemplative Prayer and the Inner Journey* 7

   Who Am I?

   How Do I Stop Talking and "Listen" to the Silence?

   Centering Prayer: A Simple Path to Contemplation

   In Silence: How Do I Do That?

   Silence and the Absence of Noise

   Centering Prayer Requires Our Consent

   Neither Resist nor Retain Any Thoughts

   What Happens during Centering Prayer?

   Engaging the Silence

   Our Human Condition: The False Self

   What Is This False Self and Where Did It Come From?

   Centering Prayer Unravels the "Homemade" False Self

   The Release of Pain: The Way to Live the Divine Plan

   Our True Self: God's Tattoo

Part 2. *Living a Contemplative Life* 41

   The God Within

   The Challenges of Centering Prayer

   The Seeds of Peace

The Circle

We Are Not Our Thoughts

Meditation Impacts Returning to Prison

Going before the Parole Board

Behind the Masks We Wear

Our Own Private Oasis

The Divine Therapy

A Mother Notices the Change

Part 3. *A Contemplative View of the Gospels* 71

The Contemplative Jesus: Model for Meditation

A Nobody Announces a Somebody

The Initiation of Jesus

Night Terror

The Parable of the Prodigal Son

A Prisoner's Reflection on the Prodigal Son

A Most Threatening Proposal

The Decontamination of the Temple

After Our Death: What Can We Expect?

To Whom Am I Indebted?

Segregated No More

Life in the Prison Wilderness

The Roofers

The Incarceration of John the Baptist

An Invitation from Christ

The Meaning of Life

The One Important Truth

The Mystery that Holds Us

Us versus Them

A Contemplative View of the Lord's Passion

The Coming of Christ Our Brother

Part 4. *Prisoner to Prisoner: Plain Talk
for Desperate Times*.. 135
Why Do You Practice Centering Prayer?
Would You Recommend Centering Prayer
to People in Prison?

Suggestions for Further Reading and Resources 141
Acknowledgments 143

About the Author
Also by Lantern Books
About the Publisher

Preface to the Third Edition

Over the last two years, more than 700 prisoners in nearly 500 prisons have written to Prison Contemplative Fellowship asking for *Finding God Within* and related materials helpful for starting contemplative groups in prison. In addition, well over a hundred prison prayer-group facilitators use *Finding God Within* as a starter handbook for contemplative prayer. I think there are two reasons for this popularity.

The first is the transformative power of centering prayer itself. It is remarkable that this gift of the Divine has been so unknown, even secret, for centuries. Yet when we are exposed to its simple methods, whether or not we have a Christian background, we recognize how personally God wants to relate to us. The methods resonate with our deeply held, often repressed, notions of how God must be in our lives.

The second reason for the book's popularity is its attunement to the experience of suffering for many prisoners. It is well known that prisoners, as a general population, have little formal education. In my view, the case is just the opposite with the personal anguish of prisoners. In this respect, most of the incarcerated have advanced degrees.

For reasons known only to God, this suffering and anguish is fertile ground for encountering a personal, even intimate, relationship with the God of Silence, the God of contemplative prayer. This is the God who has loved us from the beginning and wants nothing more than our complete wholeness and happiness. Prisoners understand this at their core. That is why many quotes from prisoners are spread throughout the book. They tell the story themselves. Who better to speak than they?

May you discover for yourself that this simple practice offers a way to a new sense of personal freedom and the deep knowledge of God.

—June 2016

I feel the Spirit of God moving me to be aware of feelings of hurt, joy, sadness, pleasure. I want to get deeper because the deeper I go, the more I have the opportunity to change.—**Harold Lawley**

Introduction
Contemplative Prayer:
A Path to Personal Transformation

Most people understand prayer to be asking God for various favors—health, safety, forgiveness, wisdom. We learn to talk to God at an early age. For many of us, the only real question as we grow older is: *Why doesn't God answer my prayers?* Because of this, many of us frequently just stop praying and hope for the best.

Contemplative prayer is an entirely different approach to prayer. It is based on God speaking to us, and all the techniques of this prayer focus on learning to listen to God's original language—Silence! This type of prayer is sometimes called *meditation* and is the type of prayer practiced in monasteries around the world. It's the deepest form of Christian prayer.

Listening to God turns out to be an extremely rewarding personal adventure. By trying to hold still we come to find out that God wants to communicate all sorts of things to us that we otherwise would not know. At the core, God wants to develop friendship with us—the friendship of a wise and loving mentor, a trusted friend who always counsels us to move toward the right path. This is an entirely new relationship with God for most people. This relationship can be both deeply rewarding and personally challenging.

As the relationship deepens, we begin to unearth parts of ourselves otherwise unknown and avoided—particularly those parts of ourselves we'd prefer not to know: our deeper fears, resentments, anger, jealousy, and the like. We also see more clearly our happiness and joy. As a result, through the techniques and effects of this type of prayer, God becomes a divine therapist who knows us intimately, loves us unconditionally, and offers us a better way to live.

We find that contemplative prayer can work well, as an eleventh step in AA. This prayer practice gets to the heart of the Big Book's invitation to "Let go and let God" by nurturing our ability to live in the present moment and just for today.

Prisoners who practice contemplative prayer can attest to the deep personal changes that come upon them. They find themselves at peace at deep levels; they feel less angry, more capable of avoiding violent responses, more willing to find positive alternatives to frustrating circumstances, and able to address life-long patterns of resentments and grief.

Contemplative prayer does not assume a particular religious faith, nor a particular prayer or Bible background. The only requirement is a willingness to explore the inner path to a relationship with God.

Definition of Terms and the Biblical Basis for Centering Prayer

The terms *meditation, contemplation, contemplative prayer,* and *centering prayer* are used interchangeably throughout this book. They are all words that describe a unique, deeply

Nothing in all creation
is so like God
as Silence.

Christian form of prayer. While there are differing root meanings for each word, they give way to a general sense of this prayer as a wordless waiting in silence for the Presence of God, as we understand God to be.

The biblical basis for centering prayer is Matthew 6:6: "When you pray [when you're looking for the right relationship with God], go to your inner room [the deep center of yourself], and pray to your Father in secret [without words], and your Father who sees in secret [is with you at your core], will reward you [grant you your heart's longing]."

* * *

Part 1 of this book deals with the notion of contemplative prayer itself: what it is, how we do it, what we can expect if we practice it, and how it makes any difference in our lives.

Part 2 is about living a daily contemplative life and the practical effects of a contemplative lifestyle. This part addresses the realities of prison life from a contemplative vantage point. It explores the spiritual journey that emerges from our prayer practice. It deals with a new awareness we develop as a result of our prayer practice. Personal experiences, up to this point hidden from us, can come into our awareness in a way previously unknown to us. Sometimes, it can appear that we're going backward in our spiritual journey. The reality is wholly different. In fact, we discover that recalling the personal traumas that emerge is a sign of progress. If we know the medicine will first make us sick and then restore us to our original sense of health, we are less likely to stop taking it. Part 2 affords a road map for the journey.

Part 3 suggests a contemplative view of the gospels. It reflects a unique way to approach the understanding of scripture and the spiritual life. It helps us gain a new perspective on what our journey means to us. As a contemplative practice takes hold for us we find that truths from the gospels are much more about changing our view of the way God works in the world than about commandments and laws of behavior. We see Jesus in a whole new light. The faith of Jesus in the Father becomes our model to see how God works in the world.

Reading scripture as a prisoner with a contemplative prayer practice brings discoveries and insights consistent with the deep knowledge of God gained in contemplation. As we find the God Within in scripture, we come to see that our morality and integrity follow almost naturally from God loving us first.

Part 4 presents prisoners describing the practice of centering prayer and its effects on them and their families. Their testimonials speak for themselves as to the power of contemplative prayer to transform one's inner self, and afford a way to navigate the realities of life in prison.

Part 1

Contemplative Prayer
and the Inner Journey

Who Am I?

If we take a good look around us, we see that we are each unique. Because we are in prison, we may have several external characteristics that look the same, but deep inside no two of us are alike. Scientists now know that our brains also form a unique pattern—no two brains, with billions of electrical impulses, are the same. No other person has the same experiences, or the same reactions to our experiences. Our inner life is deeply our own, difficult to know, and hard to talk about.

This is especially true of the dark and negative part of ourselves. This area is often off-limits for discussion in prison. Most of us go out of our way to avoid any such reflection. We march on down the line keeping any suggestion of personal change at arm's length. We let our addictions and phony self cover over and shout down the whisper of a new view of life.

Yet some of us find that in contemplative prayer God attends to our very uniqueness and communicates a certain friendship to us. We find a new confidence in our self. What comes up to us as we sit in silence appears to be exactly the exchange God desires for us, and the exchange we want as well, although we don't yet know the language of Silence.

In our quiet moments we can see the arc of our lives. We see the trajectory of our choices. We may even be able to grasp the reality that we often do what we don't want to do, and don't do what we truly want to do. Yet we seem to be able to cut ourselves some slack.

Many of us have found deep relief, even tolerance, for this desperate part of ourselves. We found this relief not by giving up our usual religious and spiritual practices. Rather, we found relief by the simple practice of resting in God. We sit without words, without promises, without shame, without even fully knowing what is happening to us, except that we have turned toward God, the Ultimate Mystery in our lives. We've learned to be still.

> God carries each person along a different road, so that you will scarcely find two people following the same route in even half of their journey to God.
> —**John of the Cross**, *The Living Flame of Love*, 3:59

How Do I Stop Talking and "Listen" to the Silence?

Wise spiritual masters through the centuries, people who are no different from ourselves, offer simple methods to come into Silence. Even before the modern discoveries of psychology and the science of how our brains work, these wise teachers found that holding still in Silence is a natural part of discovering who we are.

We have all been told, at one time or another in our lives, "Just be yourself"—even though exactly how to "be yourself" was never clear. The same suggestion applies to listening to the Silence in contemplative prayer. We are invited to do nothing, even though doing nothing is an entirely foreign notion for us. This is especially true when it comes to a relationship with God.

From our earliest years we are taught that God is watching us. We are told to do certain things, think certain things, and pray certain things to have a relationship with God. It was all up to us. Contemplative prayer offers an entirely different approach: by doing nothing, by sitting in Silence, we allow God to take over and fashion our lives as was originally intended. We begin to see God as a loving father, rather than an angry judge or abusive parent.

It is as if our inner selves naturally need a frequent vacation from the ongoing inner chatter. We have come to recognize that Silence is an essential part of our being. We don't have to do anything! The remarkable power of contemplative prayer descends on us as we do nothing. We simply have to get out of the way to allow our inner selves to find the space they are craving.

> It's like being in the eye of a storm. For that time [during centering prayer] it is being quiet in the presence of God. It allows me to quiet down when I'm flooded with words.—**Aaron Montgomery**

Centering Prayer: A Simple Path to Contemplation

Centering prayer is a simple method with easy-to-follow steps. This simple method leads us gently into resting in God, the essence of contemplative prayer.

Some of us, right at the start, found it hard to believe it could be so easy. We believed our "monkey" mind could not be denied. Yet, we too came to see that centering prayer is not about the absence of thoughts. It is, rather, about distancing or detaching from our thoughts. The term *thoughts*, by the way, refers to memories, feelings, imaginations, insights, to-do lists, our private script about our lives—all the chatter and emotions that come into our mind.

Detaching from thoughts is like watching TV in our cells. When someone comes to talk, our focus changes (detaches) from the TV. We don't listen to the TV; we may not even be aware that it's on. So it is with whatever thoughts or feelings that arise during centering prayer. We learn not to pay attention to them.

Others of us, before we tried centering prayer, were vaguely worried that this type of prayer would change our personality. We worried that somehow we'd be different in a strange way. Perhaps we thought we'd become more reclusive, less spontaneous, more pious. On other levels, some of us worried that by developing an open, listening relationship with God that God would ask something of us we simply couldn't give.

We learned that none of this is true. In fact, we found the opposite: the practice of centering prayer puts us in touch with our truest self, the self underneath so many of our false values and notions we carry around with us. We found, at the same time, a God inside who braces us on our journey. We learned that at the core we're not so bad after all; that maybe there is goodness in us that comes naturally. Centering prayer gave us back to ourselves.

In Silence: How Do I Do That?

In centering prayer our goal is to let go of all thoughts and just be in Silence, deep within us—not only not saying anything, but not intentionally thinking about anything. When we close our eyes to meditate, it is natural for all kinds of thoughts and feelings to fill our minds. We expect this: we let them come and let them go.

Here is the secret to be able to do this: before we begin the prayer, we choose a word, a simple word of one or two syllables. This becomes our "sacred word"—not in a religious way nor like a mantra used as a concentration technique, but sacred in its meaning to us. Words like *peace, love, joy, trust,* and *listen.* Some prefer *breath, life, yes, mercy,* or any word that helps us to let go of our thoughts. Then when thoughts begin to come we just repeat our sacred word silently a few times and let the thoughts go by.

This word is the only one we use in meditation. By distancing us from our thoughts, feelings, and emotions, the word serves as the symbol of our willingness, our consent, to move into our truest self—the self that opens to Presence deep within.

The use of the sacred word really hooked me in. It allows me to focus on one thing and let all other thoughts and feelings go. It's as if there is Someone else inside of me that wants me to do only His agenda.—**Steven Bell**

Silence and the Absence of Noise

Those who develop a meditation practice in prison learn early on that there is a difference between the absence of noise and Silence. There is no silence, in the usual meaning of the term, in prison. This is one of the reasons prison inmates constantly use earplugs. Silence, on the other hand, specifically Contemplative Silence, has less to do with hearing and more to do with an internal attitude about noise.

When the beginner starts a meditation practice, whether it is centering prayer or a simple stress-reduction exercise, the first great realization is how noisy our mind can be. We experience firsthand the narrative loop playing endlessly in our mind. Our recognition of the noise of our mind, and our inability to stop it on our own, makes us immediately uncomfortable and usually somewhat distressed. This is precisely why meditation is easy to explain and difficult to practice.

Centering prayer practitioners recognize that entering the realm of Silence requires a specific attitude about noise, whether around us or in our mind. Our attitude adjustment works this way. If I know that the noise from the exercise yard will surely come into the chapel, no matter what, I adjust my expectation so that I'm not surprised by it. I'm not trying by will power to keep the noise out. I can't. I simply don't pay any attention to it. The same goes for the internal noise. I choose not to notice it. Experienced practitioners remark that they often do not actually hear the noise when they are engaging in centering prayer.

When someone comes to our cell to talk, the conversation itself doesn't turn down the volume of the TV. Our focus on the conversation does. In the meditation practice of centering prayer, we are taught to use our breath or a sacred word to re-focus the noise in our mind, i.e., the continuous thoughts passing through us. Increasingly, the noise moves off into the distance. It's still noise but we somehow incorporate it into our attitude toward Silence. It's still there, but we've gone to another place. The Place of Silence.

The Place of Silence has even less to do with noise. Here, words are no longer necessary or helpful. We are simply "present" to the deep interior stillness of our being. Some call this remarkable journey inside "finding God within."

This experience of sitting still, this internal quietness, is beyond my ability to express. It simply must be ventured into by an open-minded participant. We are each unique and priceless. Centering Prayer gives me a great sense of my relationship with God.
—**Angel Estelle**

Centering Prayer Requires Our Consent

Consent is the heart and soul of centering prayer. This one word can summarize the entirety of this profound spiritual practice. Yet it is easy for us to miss the significance of our consent.

The essence of the prayer is based on mutual agreement. This is not some phony plea-bargain where you have no real choice. This agreement is based in freedom, yours and God's. Think about it this way: imagine a contract. Both parties have to agree, otherwise there is no binding agreement, no contract. So it is with the Divine. God wants to fill us with God's own life by becoming present to us and working in our lives. To do this without our consent would be to overpower us and take away our freedom. This is not the God of centering prayer.

Our use of the sacred word is a shortcut, an almost mechanical reminder that our intention is to consent to God being present and active in our lives. We know that holding still allows God's presence and action to take over.

In other words, we detach from our usual internal dialogue—with all its judgments, storylines, hidden hurts, and prejudices—and let God's Silence do the talking. Using our sacred word we simply and gently move into an entirely different space in our ongoing relationship with God. God is doing the initiating. Our job is to agree (consent) to his presence and action in our lives.

We soon see that our sacred word represents our deepest intention to be open to the divine life within us. This intention of ours is more valuable than the craziness of our attention. This willingness to be quiet with Presence allows the divine life already within to move us deeper.

With stillness comes acceptance. Acceptance brings a letting-go to our core. Personal change begins in earnest.

> The desire to go to God, to open to His presence within us, does not come from our initiative. We do not have to go anywhere to find God because He is already drawing us in every conceivable way into union with Himself. It is rather a question of opening to an action that is already happening in us. To consent to God's presence *is* His Presence.
> —**Thomas Keating**, *Open Mind, Open Heart,* p. 46

How to Do Centering Prayer

1. Before you begin, choose a sacred word* as a symbol of your intention to consent to the presence and action of God within you.
2. Sit comfortably, close your eyes, and begin to settle down. Take a few deep, slow breaths to help you relax and stay loose. Recall your intention to consent to the presence and action of God within you, and then silently introduce your sacred word.

3. When you get caught up in your thoughts,** return ever-so-gently to your sacred word.
4. At the end of your prayer time, remain seated and relaxed for a couple of minutes while you slowly open your eyes and begin to move.

* Your sacred word can be a simple word of one or two syllables or it can be your breath or it can be both. Words like *peace*, *love*, *joy*, *trust*, and *listen* are good. Some prefer *breath*, *life*, *yes*, *mercy*, *God*, *Jesus*, or any word that helps us to let go of our thoughts without creating new thoughts. If you use your breath, you simply notice that you are breathing in and out without trying to change how you're breathing. To use both, you might silently say your sacred word as you breathe in and out. Whatever we choose becomes our "sacred symbol," not in a religious way, nor like a mantra used as a concentration technique, but sacred in how it expresses our consent.

** Thoughts refer to any idea, feeling, emotion, memory, physical sensation, image, reflection, plan, opinion, or spiritual experience that comes to awareness.

Some Practical Points

It is normal and natural for all kinds of thoughts to come. During the prayer time, let thoughts come and let thoughts go. When you have trouble letting thoughts go, gently return to your sacred word until the thoughts go by.

Set aside a time for your practice, twice a day if possible. Twenty minutes is the goal for a period of centering prayer, but do what is feasible. Times prior to count or chow work well for many. It helps to use a timer as long as the timer is not so loud as to make you jump when it goes off.

Find a sitting position that is comfortable for you to remain still for 20 minutes. Whatever position you use, keep the back straight. For many, it is easier to sit without moving if your back is supported.

The main fruits of centering prayer occur in our daily lives, not during our prayer periods.

Neither Resist nor Retain Any Thoughts

After a period of time, we learn that we cannot stop thoughts, or other feelings, from coming up during meditation. They simply arise on their own. Any forced attempt through will power (*I'm not going to think or feel that . . .*) simply doesn't work. We learn not to be surprised by any manner of thoughts or intense feelings coming during centering prayer. We don't resist them.

Because they can carry us away from our Silence, we use the sacred word to release them. Our deep selves know that retaining these thoughts or feelings just takes us out of our Silence, and leaves us with the same old story of our lives.

As we learn centering prayer, we come upon a truly remarkable discovery: this practical prayer method, detaching from our thoughts, is the key to our own freedom in our daily life. It is like a duck raised as a chicken. The duck never knew swimming came naturally until he found himself in water! The simple act of doing nothing and being nothing (no thing) as we sit in God's presence frees us to be the unique person we were created to be.

Centering prayer is the cornerstone of contemplative commitment. This prayer creates the space of openness and receptivity where God actively participates by living our life for us, and we become a conduit for Divine Energy to move into the world.
—**Thomas Keating**, *Centering Prayer*

The best part of centering prayer for me is to just sit and say my sacred word. I know I could ask God for anything, but I just sit and know that God loves and cares for me.—**Gilbert Seranno**

When I do centering prayer I can spend time in eternity so that the small things in the temporary world are not so hard to deal with. When all the "boats" (my thoughts) go by, carrying all my feelings and pain, and I don't get on the boat, I'm on the eternity side. But the greatest thing for me with this practice is that now I'm not afraid to approach God.
—**Lawrence Hamilton**

What Happens during Centering Prayer?

As in any relationship, the more time we spend with the other person, the more we come to know him or her. Our experience is no different with the God of our understanding, except it is harder to talk about it. Because we enter into Silence, no words can describe the experience. We become aware of God's presence and action in our lives; but talking about them can be extremely difficult.

For some, the experience is like a vast, empty space of tranquility and safety. For other people, the experience is like a cloud descending on them. This description is not new. One of the first books on this type of prayer was written by an anonymous author in the fourteenth century. It is called *The Cloud of Unknowing*, and you'll notice that it's not called *The Cloud of **Not**-knowing*. We learn plenty about ourselves, particularly our hidden, repressed selves. Our "knowing" is in the gut, not the head.

As we sit in centering prayer, distancing ourselves from our words and thoughts, we find that immediate evaluations of our prayer practice are not helpful. It's like asking fish to describe their experience of water! As a result, we don't judge our periods of centering prayer as "good" or "bad" by the times we use our sacred word or the amount of distractions we encounter. Similarly, we recognize that our experience of Presence is not dependent on feeling God's presence.

As a method of meditation, Centering Prayer is founded upon the gesture of surrender, or letting go. The theological basis for this prayer lies in the principle of *kenosis* (Philippians 2:6), Jesus' self-emptying love that forms the core of his own self-understanding and life practice. During the prayer time itself, surrender is practiced through the letting go of thoughts as they arise. Unlike other forms of meditation, neither focused awareness nor a steady witnessing presence is required. There is no need to "follow" the thoughts as they arise; merely to let them go promptly as soon as you realize you're engaged in thinking (a "Sacred Word" is typically used to facilitate this prompt release).

—**Cynthia Bourgeault**, *Centering Prayer and Inner Awakening*, p. 162

Engaging the Silence

As centering prayer becomes a regular practice, as we "rest in God" free of preconceived words or notions of what we need from God, gradually our rigid defenses begin to change. Our usual thought-patterns and ways we experience consciousness start to shift. At first, we are surprised to see the shift and wonder, *When did I start thinking this?* Or, *I haven't thought about that painful event in years!*

These thoughts and images arise as much outside centering prayer time, in our daily life, as during our prayer time. Since we detach ourselves during prayer time, and feel no urgency to process the narrative during that period, we find the experience comes up during our daily routines. Our prayer practice has loosened deeply embedded experiences.

For those who are not familiar with these effects of centering prayer, it can feel like we are going backward into events and storylines we thought we had overcome. Here we are, for example, feeling lost in grief or anger, when we thought we had everything under control. If not recognized as progress, this can be severely discouraging: *Why do I always feel like I've screwed up?*

Patience helps us to see that this discouragement comes from our bogus view of what it means to be a man. Society would have us believe we should avoid all our painful experiences at any cost. Yet in meditation we learn we are freeing ourselves from our constant storyline streaming in our mind, and we are actually learning something new about ourselves.

We discover that some of the routines in our lives—the music, TV, games, and so forth—serve as a way of avoiding these very experiences. Feeling and seeing them now is actually a good thing. The space we create in centering prayer, as we detach from thinking, now is the space we need to encounter our deeper selves—the material lodged in our unconsciousness. We have newfound personal freedom. We know ourselves in a way not known before.

While remembering and reliving past memories may seem strange at first, we come to see that this is the direct route to personal healing and change. It's the type of transformation we always vaguely knew we needed, but simply didn't have the means to get there. We come face to face with our false self.

> Centering prayer allows me to deal with all those events and memories that I have chosen to avoid, especially the painful and shameful ones. I find as I deal with them, little by little, they lose their power over me.—**Daniel Delgado**

Our Human Condition: The False Self

As the human family has developed and evolved over time, we have learned that much of our personal experience, particularly the deeply painful events of our childhood, is buried deep within our own personal unconscious, separate from our conscious awareness and seemingly inaccessible to our rational will power.

This personal unconscious contains all the self-serving habits that have been woven into our personality from the time we were conceived; all the emotional damage that has come from our early environment and upbringing; all the harm that other people have done to us knowingly or unknowingly at an age when we could not defend ourselves.

Also in this deep, secret part of ourselves are the methods, the programs for happiness, we acquired at an early age to protect and defend ourselves to ward off the pain of unbearable situations. It makes sense that we develop these methods as infants because our survival is at stake. The strategies are all about our basic needs for survival, esteem, affection, power, and control. Because these plans started when we were infants, we think that they're actually part of our "self." Unfortunately, these unconscious programs that we needed to survive when we were defenseless don't hold up in a world of seven billion other people competing for the same things. That's why these happiness plans are called "false," not "bad."

The early false-self methods grow into sources of motivation for happiness. They are made much more complex as we grow into adulthood, and reinforced by our social environment, our parents, neighborhood, schools, churches, and the like.

The heart of the struggle with our false self—that part of ourselves that does what we don't want, and doesn't do what we do want—addresses our unconscious motivations for happiness. If we do not recognize these hidden influences, the false self will simply adjust to our "new" way of life and nothing really changes. Even if we commit to Christ, we still pursue our need for security, success, and power—only this time in a Christian context. The false self unconsciously follows us into whatever lifestyle we choose.

The good news is this: we can find happiness, and relief from our false self, by looking in different places. As we become more aware of these false programs, we begin to see our unhappiness is in our false plans—not in our self or how others treat us.

My first experiences with centering prayer were boring. But over time I realized that it began to give me more control over how I responded to all of life's situations. It allows me to see why living in the chaos of our addictive thinking never achieves any enlightenment at all. The best part of the practice is the self-control and insights. I have found I have patience and forgiveness for the "failings" of others.—**Harvey Jacobs**

What Is This False Self and Where Did It Come From?

The false self describes the self we make to cope with the emotional experiences of early childhood. We came into our world with instinctual needs to stay alive. Our instincts tell us, even before we can think, that we need food and tenderness from our mothers. Our basic instincts teach us to cry when we need help—all this from the moment we are born.

As we grow, our basic instincts grow more complex. Our physical and emotional needs become more complicated as we begin to think on our own. These needs develop in the context of family and neighborhood, which have their own particular view and idea for meeting these basic human needs. When these needs aren't satisfied when we are young, without our realizing it we make our own programs to satisfy these needs. Some call this false self the "homemade" self—it's the best we can do with our inner experience. We do it because we believe that our very survival is at stake, and in some inner sense, it *is*.

This "homemade" false self is subtly influenced by early childhood trauma. These traumas are common for all of us. They have little to do with the intentions of the adults around us. All we know as children is that our mother may not come to us when we cry or that we should be afraid of our father. We may be exposed to, or directly experience, abusive events so painful we unwittingly dump them immediately into our unconscious. These early childhood traumas, combined with our unmet instinctual childhood needs, supply the energy and driving force of our adult attempts at happiness.

What happens next makes a lot of sense: we invent a self necessary to address these losses. If we didn't receive the affection we craved as a child, we'll look for it everywhere as an adult: we look for a wife who will treat us like she is our mother. Or, we'll be the best athlete at any cost to get the recognition we never felt from our father. Through centering prayer we come to see that these attempts at happiness won't meet the need that created them.

> Centering prayer has taught me how to resist feelings of anger that come from officers and inmates. In my time of silence I have learned to dump my trash and let God fill my life with his peace. Our trash can be very hurting and confusing if we don't understand it is the false self talking and not your comforting God.—**Harold Lawley**

Centering Prayer Unravels the "Homemade" False Self

As centering prayer becomes a frequent practice for us, the motives of our false self become noticeable. We begin to find our homemade selves everywhere! The concrete wall separating our conscious thinking from our unconscious buried material, developed over a lifetime, begins to crumble because of our centering prayer practice. The power of our false self that originates in our unconscious becomes observable. Those memories, too painful to feel, hidden in our unconscious, begin slowly to emerge.

This happens more in our daily life than during prayer. All of a sudden we remember long-forgotten events. This time, they appear with a certain perspective that has space around it similar to the space we create around the thoughts and feelings that arise during centering prayer. The space supplies that particular quality in our gut that attracts us to the event in ways we have never experienced before. We feel less afraid.

While the event may still hold the sting of the long-ago repression, we somehow find the courage to let it come into our full consciousness. We learn to let it teach us what it wants to teach us. Our willingness to stay with the memory allows us to be present to it in a way we have never been able to do. Much of our inner experience lies beyond words and concepts so we have a hard time finding words to describe this, even to ourselves. Yet we know that deep movement is happening within.

Usually, for the first time, we grasp how entirely self-centered our plans actually are. We learn that we have placed ourselves at the center of the universe, as if the world exists to meet our needs, and have asked God to kindly go along with our plans. Of course, this is exactly opposite to reality, and opposite to the true way that happiness can come to us. We learn from hard-won experience that we have it upside down and inside out. True happiness comes to us not in a self-centered world, but in a world that has our experience of the Divine plan in the center.

> The power of centering prayer has granted me the courage to face the demonic forces of lies that deceived me from childhood until today. It gives me the confidence to confront and discern the lies that I face within and from without on a daily basis.
> —**Aaron Montgomery**
>
> The fruits of this practice are obvious when you compare the attitudes of those who practice centering prayer with those of the general prison population. . . . I think God speaks to us subtly in our lives. If we aren't listening we might miss it or even doubt his existence. Centering prayer is a stubborn child who patiently sits before the Father not to be ignored, waiting to feel His love.
> —**Paul Dietering**

The Release of Pain: The Way to Live the Divine Plan

The letting-go part of centering prayer steps forward to help us change our self-centered view of life. Although we maintain our separation from thoughts and feelings as we do centering prayer, the benefits are most available in our daily life. We are able to enter a room deep inside, even though it had been locked up tight, bolted, and nailed shut. The door swings open! The denials and avoidances in our lives begin to surface naturally on their own. As we walk the yard we remember an act of kindness to us we hadn't thought about in years. We begin to grasp patterns of behavior throughout our lives that have caused us pain, anger, and grief. We see the sunset in a way we'd never noticed before.

As our psychological material of a lifetime rises to the surface, we witness a new sense of self emerging on its own that neutralizes the pain. From somewhere deep inside, we begin to say: *Maybe I'm more OK than I ever thought. Maybe God does love me, the* real *me.*

As we rest deeper in God in contemplation, ever-so-subtly our self-image begins to change and shift. Feelings, memories, painful recollections—all the hidden material of a lifetime—start to discharge naturally into our awareness: sometimes as a gentle stream, at other times a tidal wave.

The vast storeroom of our traumatized self is opening to divine therapy: a gentle encounter that allows us to patiently mull over the experience of a lifetime. (See p. 64.)

We recognize a subtle principle at work in our contemplative practice: there is an unmistakable connection between experiencing traumatic events in our past and a sense of our own deep, at-the-core goodness. "Made in the image of God" takes on new meaning for us in our gut as well as our mind. We discover we actually possess the humility and courage for the personal change we crave. We find we experience hope at deep levels, hope that allows us to continue our spiritual journey in earnest.

Our True Self: God's Tattoo

When we first become familiar with notions of the false self and the havoc we see it create in our lives, we can't get rid of it enough. We'll do anything to build up our true selves.

But as we progress in our prayer practice, we discover something different. Our true self is already with us. It lies buried underneath the programs and projects created by our desperate search for happiness.

We don't have to empty the bottle before we can fill it. We learn that our truest self is a natural, God-given orientation waiting to be tapped and released from our inner self. As we watch our futile attempts to hang onto our plans for security, esteem, and control, we more readily see how useless they are. We see our fierce grip on anger begin to loosen. We observe our own activities with a newfound objectivity that allows us to see our part in relationship struggles: *Maybe I actually did have something to do with this conflict.*

When we get caught again in the activities and motives of our false self, as we frequently do, we return to our prayer practice for reorientation. We find compassion coming out of us without our even thinking about it. We begin to see ourselves in the people around us, even the guards. (*Looks like he is having a bad day.*) We find that we can cut people some slack in a way we couldn't do before.

The space developed in centering prayer gives us a freedom rarely experienced before. Our ability to let go of conflicting emotions during prayer allows us to let go of them in our daily life. This spaciousness brings us, without effort, into a greater awareness of the enormity of the present moment. The goals and outcomes of our plans seem less important. We find now that we can actually live in the "present moment" in a fashion we didn't know before.

Now we understand the old adage:

> *The past is over,*
> *the future is not here,*
> *I have only the present.*

Our experience tells us that the present moment holds everything for us. The true self emerges from within ourselves. It doesn't come suddenly, like turning on a light switch. It is a gradual birth of a part of ourselves long buried. This part of us is the DNA of God in our lives. This is what is meant by the "image" of God. It is the spot where God has forever tattooed us with God's own specially recognized sign that we belong to God. Now when we are undecided about a course of action in our lives, holding still in the present moment unlocks enormous potential. The butterfly is emerging from the cocoon. Nothing will be the same again.

I don't have the opportunity to talk to other inmates in the SHU [Security Housing Unit], so centering prayer and the Contemplative Fellowship are really important to me. My spirit is free . . . and I am always with you during your Monday-night meetings.

—**Luis Suastegui**

The centering prayer class lets me take time to focus on my spiritual journey. I love this class because it teaches us to stop trying to please our false self and begin to feel fulfilled. I feel closer to my Spiritual Destination then ever in my 32-year-old life.

—**G. Rodriquez**

The purpose of . . . [entering into silence] is to sink into the invincible conviction of being loved by God, loved simply because one has become aware of one's own desperate need and of one's complete dependence on God.—**Thomas Keating**, *Reflections on the Unknowable*, p. 134

Part 2
Living a Contemplative Life

Our weekly gathering for centering prayer and discussions on the contemplative journey are essential to our prayer practice. In the meeting, we listen to one another and learn that no two of us have exactly the same spiritual journey. We look the same, dress the same, and go through the same daily routines, yet we see and hear in our meetings that the Divine works with us in personally distinctive ways.

Some of us are immediately thrust into an awareness of the pain in which we live. Once we turn off our headphones and TVs and try to go inside ourselves free of distractions, we are surrounded and immersed in the very pain we have tried to avoid. Our pain seems to emerge from a lifetime of disappointments and poor decisions, like a drain that is backing up. We have a whole new awareness of the addictions that have driven so many of our decisions.

For others, the awareness is like stepping into the sunshine after years of darkness and cold. We find joy and satisfaction in the smallest of things. Seeing a friend in the yard, receiving a casual letter from home, remembering someone long-forgotten—these seem to bring us a deeper sense of peace than previously we'd known.

We recognize in our meetings that our lives now are a mixture of joy and pain. We learn that no experience, no matter what it is, has the power to completely and finally take away the access we've gained to our inmost self. Once afflicted, we have only to reach into our prayer practice to contact our self and the spaciousness now awaiting us there. We find that our practice of contemplative prayer is portable. We take it with us wherever we go: our cell, the SHU, the yard, wherever.

As individual as our journey is, we find out that we practitioners are a lot alike. That is why we call our group Prison Contemplative Fellowship. The companionship we experience together—free of economic, educational, and racial boundaries—is like few associations we have in prison.

I look forward to the group circle and the different ethnic backgrounds of the group. We all understand that we are in a safe environment. The safety and security of the group still remain the same after all these years.

My practice of centering prayer gives me a deep awareness of the "balance" of God's creation—gifts of warmth and cold, the seasons, the colors. Even in the darkness and loneliness of prison, Centering can take me to good places.—**William Hays**

The God Within

The goal of contemplative prayer, of "waiting on God," or the promise of "resting in God" through a practice of centering prayer, seems strange and awkward at first. What is this "waiting" or "resting"? Isn't our relationship with God mainly about "doing" and "acting" in a way consistent with God's commandments?

Actually, resting in God (contemplative prayer) invites us to a wholly different relationship with the Ultimate Mystery we call *God* and Jesus called *Father*.

For most of our early life, our view of God is unconscious and unexamined. The God of our youth, taught to us as children in these years, in hundreds of subtle ways and for many reasons, through our Churches, teachers, parents, and our own fantasies, looks very much like any other authority figure! If we've had problems with authority figures we tend to imagine similar problems with God. Our thoughts of God may be positive, even loving, but in the back of our minds we know this God has the upper hand, absolute power, and control of everything, and is always watching us.

Scripture describes another view, and contemplative prayer gives us a method. Jesus' most frequent commandment to his followers when speaking about God is: *Do not be afraid!* For Jesus, it is not about reacting in fear to this powerful God, but opening to the Divine Presence already waiting for us deep inside.

This is the point of Jesus' Parable of the Prodigal Son (see p. 83). It is a good starting point for centering prayer practice. This is the God Within and the deepest driving force in Jesus. His stories constantly challenge his listeners to throw off the God-to-be-afraid-of and accept a different view of God. We need to listen and do the same.

Instead of trying to impress and earn the respect of this controlling God, we need to look inside and accept the invitations from the God that loves us, as one wise person says, "no matter what." Instead of counting our material goods and thanking this God for blessing and rewarding us, we examine our relationship with this loving God and realize the blessings of the "poor in spirit" and the "meek and merciful" (Matthew 5:3–12).

This actual awareness of God as Father is the promise of contemplative prayer and the value of the practice of centering prayer.

> My centering prayer practice draws me closer to God because it helps me feel one with God. It's like I finally know where I belong and what my relationship with God is supposed to be. I realize it is my spiritual journey with God, and nobody else's.
> —Jeff Clay

The Challenges of Centering Prayer

The practical obstacles to doing centering prayer are many and obvious. Starting any new practice demands, at the very least, a decision to change our comfortable routines and familiar ways of living life.

Somewhere in the back of our minds the practice of centering prayer can bring a vague fear of silence and what may lie beyond and within this silence. Sometimes doing centering prayer just seems boring! When we enter our traditional way of praying, at least we know what we're praying for; at least we know what we are putting before the God we believe in. But with centering prayer we can sometime get a hazy thought that God may ask something of us we are not willing to do. Or, we will have no experience of God whatsoever.

The fear, actually, makes a lot of sense because in centering prayer we are going into our own wilderness, and, on some level, allowing ourselves to experience our personal loneliness, broken relationships, and failures. If we make a habit of hiding these realities from others and from ourselves, of course any change in our patterns will create a sense of anxiety and fear.

In the beginning, our curiosity will help us overcome these initial fears and anxieties of a new relationship with

God. As we progress, and experience God at deeper levels, courage and determination will keep us going.

Prisoners do overcome these initial fears and start a centering prayer practice. We start for various reasons: some because we want to change the direction of our spiritual lives, others because we want to try something besides words. We experience a kind of curiosity about this different type of prayer where words are less important and "listening" is emphasized.

As we develop a meditation practice, our routine consciousness expands to include seemingly irresolvable conflicts in our relationships. We appear to experience conflicts with a new awareness. For example, we think, *How can I continue to have an active relationship with my daughter when her mother doesn't want her to have contact with me?* Now, instead of going off on how poisonous her mother is relative to us, we can truly appreciate her point of view. We seem to gain a "space" around the conflict that contains more appreciation for complexity, with greater patience for finding an outcome consistent with that complexity. This "space" (what some masters call "the Spaciousness of the Divine") contains alternatives and strategies we hadn't yet anticipated.

We discover in our difficulties with centering prayer that, as with other self-development tools, hidden and unrealistic expectations can do us in. These expectations grow like lawn weeds: they're hard to see at first, but if left to grow unrecognized they can take over the patch. If we can view these expectations directly, we can treat them as any other thought during centering prayer. Treating these excessive expectations in this fashion reduces their energy and lessens their control over us.

Every time I try to meditate I hear all the noise around me, I get angry, and I can't get myself still to even say my sacred word.—**W.M.**

After nearly 40 years of incarceration I certainly did not believe I possessed the ability to meditate. The thought of relinquishing trust to someone produced anxiety, insecurity, and disbelief. But today I'm good to a point. I still harbor many trust issues, but through my meditation practice I'm working continuously to overcome these emotions.
—**Shorty Cavanaugh**

The Seeds of Peace

The practice of meditation (centering prayer) is an invitation to deep, personal freedom. The obstacles to developing a meditation practice are the very same obstacles to developing our sense of personal freedom. We are drawn to meditation as we are drawn to any practice (spiritual, physical, emotional) that promises to give us relief from that deep, nagging, negative self—the continuing experience of being less than who we truly are and who we want to be.

Yet, we are surprised when our first experiences in meditation bring up parts of ourselves we are trying to forget: our anger, fear, jealousy, sense of competition, and pride. These emotions are usually embedded in the stories that come as we sit to meditate. We begin with our sacred word and immediately we are annoyed at the level of noise around us, or we remember how disappointed we are that someone did not pay sufficient attention to us or disrespected us. Then we find ourselves back years ago, when a teacher humiliated us or a parent yelled and shamed us for reasons we don't recall. Now we feel worse than before we began to meditate. Some of us ask: *Why would I want to meditate only to have these painful experiences emerge in my mind? Aren't I trying to not remember these things? Isn't "not remembering" what peace is all about?*

Inmates who have overcome these beginning obstacles to a meditation practice tell us that there is a critical added ingredient as we sit and endure these painful memories: we feel some vague sense that we are more than that person in the story. We are not *only* that humiliated and shamed child; there is something more to us than all our negative, mental narratives suggest. What can this ingredient be? As we gently return to the sacred word, we let these painful memories arise and fade away, aware they may come again. We trust that there are other, deeper parts of ourselves that give us courage to face our shame and fear. Slowly and gradually this trust emerges as an experience: *Maybe the Divine does actually love me after all! Maybe I'm a lot more than that humiliated child.*

These are the "seeds" of peace. This is the draw of meditation that invites us to a profound freedom that is totally our own, not based on opinions or judgments from others. These seeds come from our deepest Self and are the lasting gift of a meditation practice.

> Through the practice of centering prayer a miraculous transformation takes place that I have not experienced in any other spiritual practice. In my opinion, it seems that this transformation can only happen through contact with God's divine grace and love. Centering prayer is a conduit to God's love and caring nature. Given time, the manifestation of these principles is tangible.—**Michael Fairfax**

It's all about "the Circle" for me during lockdown. I see The Boat picture and it reminds me of the circle we sit in when we meditate on Monday nights. It gives me strength to continue to open myself to God's presence.—**William Hays**

The Circle

The Prison Contemplative Fellowship is a community of prisoners, former prisoners, their families, chaplains, and volunteers who practice centering prayer. It is a fellowship that recognizes our individuality and celebrates our unique relationship with the Divine.

Prisoners find that sending centering prayer materials home to their loved ones opens new channels of communication and understanding as to the personal transformations developing within them.

Meditating alone in our cells can seem like an inner, self-centered act that has no impact whatsoever on anyone else. In fact, much of the language that teaches meditation and contemplative prayer focuses on our uniqueness and the individual ways the Divine Healer works in our life.

This is one of the extraordinary parts of contemplative prayer. We need rely on no one for our meditation practice. Lockdowns, in some respects, make it even easier to do our meditation. We have fewer choices to distract us.

There is another view: a contemplative practice brings outside, other-centered movement. The Divine Healer works with us individually, for sure. Yet there is no doubt that God entrusts us to one another in similarly healing ways. We hear helpful remarks from someone in the group; they give us helpful suggestions on how to deal with various parts of a meditation practice; or, they talk about their own inner journey in a way that opens for us a deeper appreciation of our own journey. We find ourselves sitting in amazement at the wisdom coming from another prisoner.

At other times, someone can be unaware of the ways they inspire us. A simple act of kindness can have a profound impact on our awareness and create in us a desire to go deeper into our practice. We become present to each other in the Silence. We come to understand that our impact on one another is not coincidental.

> Praying in a group has had more meaning for me than doing it alone. I am amazed at the transformation that occurs, and the depth of spiritual wisdom and commitment. Meditation with the Fellowship is exciting and unbelievably sincere.
> —**Frank Brown**, volunteer

We Are Not Our Thoughts

The simple technique of movement away from thoughts and feelings during meditation by use of the sacred word demonstrates for us a revolutionary notion: we are not our thoughts. We find many of our self-inflicted, false self–dominated conflicts are the product of a never-ending mental commentary on the people and events around us.

When we experience the separation between our selves and our "thoughts," we tend to let ourselves off the hook of negative self-judgments. We begin ever-so-subtly to realize that we are not as badly off as we sometimes feel, or as some people tell us we are.

We also begin to notice a space between our thoughts and our choices for action. In fact, sometimes we can see that no matter the thought, even a thought that triggers some deep emotion in us, we don't have to do anything. Something valuable happens inside of us when we don't do anything! This notion is really foreign to much of the so-called wisdom of the day that says we must be "forceful men of action" or "decisive" or "leaders."

This discipline of not identifying with our thoughts is the foundation of the new awareness we find in ourselves outside of meditation. It's as if we find new breathing room for the multiple thoughts and emotions we carry with us all the time.

The quiet and deep movements inside of us, usually kept in the background, now have room to express themselves. The "space" that we discovered in centering prayer now provides the meeting place for us to deal with ourselves in a new and creative way: *When did I start thinking about that? How is it I'm not inclined to do this anymore? This "personal" conflict is really not about me.*

The simple exercise of releasing thoughts as they arise in centering prayer has an enormous pay-off in our lives. It is the key to a personal freedom that cannot be taken away, or prohibited, or locked down.

All methods that lead to contemplation are more or less aimed at bypassing the thinking process. The reason is that our thinking process tends to reinforce our addictive process—our frenzy to "get something" from the outer world to fuel our compulsions or to mask our pain. If we can just rest on a regular basis for twenty to thirty minutes without thinking, we begin to see that we are not our thoughts. We *have* thoughts, but we are not our thoughts. Most people suffer because they think that they are their thoughts and if their thoughts are upsetting, distressing, or evil, they are stuck with them. If they just stopped thinking for a while every day as a discipline, they would begin to see that they do not have to be dominated by their thoughts.—**Thomas Keating**, *Intimacy with God*, pp. 68–69

Meditation Impacts Returning to Prison

It is well known in the criminal-justice literature that the practice of meditation is a critical factor in whether a prisoner will return to prison after release. The research seems to indicate that this fact is true no matter the type of meditation practice. Why?

Centering prayer meditation practice says it like this: when we sit in silence for 20 minutes twice a day, we begin to make two important discoveries in daily life. The first is that God actually loves and cares for us. This realization is not like turning on a light switch. It's an experience that comes less noticeably, but often quickly. It may come in a chow line or in the yard. Early on, the meditator begins to realize we actually do have our own specific and unique relationships with God, and God does seem to be taking an interest in us.

The second discovery is connected to the first. Practitioners begin to understand and appreciate the poor decisions they made in their life. This discovery arises free of guilt and shame, in a way that meditators can actually begin to see their lives with new eyes. It's like a review of your life in a relaxed conversation with a friend whose opinion you really trust. We know that our friend has always had our best interests at heart. We can listen without retaliating.

Centering prayer calls this experience the "unloading of the unconscious" because it is an un-loading (a natural emergence) of materials we've held within ourselves for a lifetime. It is really an unburdening of our deepest secrets in a way that allows them to emerge into the light of day. When it does reach the surface it comes into the setting of acceptance and compassion like a relaxed conversation with a friend. We can actually view our personal experience without drowning in self-hatred and self-contempt.

When we experience this unloading during centering prayer and return to our sacred word, we experience the actual freeing of ourselves from a lifetime of torment and self-loathing. Somehow we are saying to ourselves that, *Yes, this may be true, but it is not the whole story. There is much more to me than this.*

From this point of view, personal problems are easier to see and resolve. Behavior that arises out of deep personal turmoil is seen for what it is. We are now more likely to treat ourselves with respect and compassion. We have the habit of going into our spaciousness where personal choices are unlimited, and we recognize that returning to prison is a poor choice among a host of positive ones.

> Meditation is a call to salvation and resurrection for me. Without it, I'm in the desert fighting for my life, under attack from within.—**Aaron Montgomery**

I came to centering prayer class for help and insight in dealing with feelings about life. I guess I needed to be OK with being not OK.

For me, the practice of contemplative prayer means a never-ending journey. There is always some new breakthrough. Everything that is not you and not God disappears into what is God or God's love. When I come out of meditation I feel like I bring more of God's love back with me.

—**Lawrence Hamilton**

Going before the Parole Board

Many of the prisoners in the centering prayer circle find that this unloading of the unconscious material within is helpful in preparing for testimony before their parole board. This is true for several reasons.

The first reason is that every week in the circle the talk focuses on why we do the things we do—even the things we don't want to do, the things that cause all the trouble. We learn that the standard explanations no longer work. We see that our general awareness at the time was so limited we couldn't possibly understand all the deep experiences we carried with us. We begin to understand that long-forgotten memories, too painful to keep in mind, stay in our personal unconscious and continue to influence our decisions.

Here is what is going on: as the repressed material of our lives gently emerges in our centering prayer practice, we get a new view of the deep and subtle forces working us when we committed the criminal acts that landed us in prison. The parole board wants to know if we understand why we did what we did. Using the language of the unloading of the unconscious gives us an objective means of describing the crimes, yet it also allows us to speak personally, from the inside. Prisoners can take responsibility for their actions in a new and more sincere way because they know how to describe the factors at play in their lives at the time.

This is not some new pose that tricks the board. It is one of the first fruits of a centering prayer practice: we have a new vision of who we are now and who we were when we committed the crimes that bring us before the board. It's a strange combination of new and old: the new person can see exactly how the old person was being worked by his prior experiences, particularly those long repressed from childhood. With a newfound compassion for ourselves we can own up to motives we did not comprehend at the time. By doing this, we can explain the crime with knowledge and compassion for the victims, and, just as importantly, for ourselves.

Behind the Masks We Wear

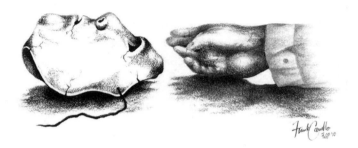

In classical times actors wore masks on stage. The audience could readily see, by the mask, the emotion (and maybe even the intentions) of the actors. The Latin word for this mask is the origin of our word *person*. Notice it isn't the real inside emotion or intention of the actor, only the mask. By birth and training we are all "actors" in this sense. We wear various masks for various situations. Over time, we begin to believe that the mask we wear is actually who we are! We think it is our authentic self.

As we start a spiritual practice like centering prayer, we begin to see the person behind the mask. In the beginning this can be upsetting, even terrifying: *Is there this much falseness in me? Is there anything of me beyond the mask?* We launch more seriously into the realm of the false self in action.

Actually, it is not only the false self that we see. It is really greater self-knowledge we are gaining, not just the uselessness of the false masks we wear. Our newfound ability to see the excessive strivings for security/survival, affection/esteem, and control/power means we have developed a deeper degree of self-awareness. As some men put it: our consciousness is expanding.

We see the mask because, at the same time, somewhere inside we know our "trueness." We need not be discouraged by the size and depth of our false self (not the bad self) or the many subtle ways the false self is injected into our intentions and actions. Something "true" is emerging at a deeper level.

Once we become aware of the masks we wear, the simple sitting in stillness of a practice like centering prayer gives us the needed strength of heart, the courage, to move through our experience of falseness. We somehow find a way, or a "way" is given to us, to move on and through our experience of falseness.

Though we rarely experience it at the time, in truth as we reflect back on our change in awareness we begin to see the work of the divine healer and the remarkable emergence of our true self. The transformation of the self now begins in earnest.

> The same emotions that trap us in our unhappiness are guides to the transcendent. It all depends on how we view them—as resistance to change in our personal status quo or as invitations to surrender our ego control. These emotions are hints that there is something immeasurably more to life than what I've yet discovered or experienced.—**Gregory Mayers**, *Listen to the Desert*, p. 39

Our Own Private Oasis

Listening to prisoners with a centering prayer practice we seem to agree that our meditation creates some sort of quiet oasis in the midst of the noise and intensity of living in prison. We are able to go to this oasis despite the clamor and blare of TV and music. For many of us, this quiet place is the goal of meditation. We find respite here free from the madness surrounding us in prison.

This oasis is an ever-expanding inner space that is the place where we meet our truest self. This space has great depth and it increases as we develop the habit of meditation. Several experiences emerge here.

The first is the awareness that events of our day, particularly those of conflict, are not meant to be taken personally. We get a sense that whatever is confronting us is not really about us! It may be about whatever is bothering the person we meet. We somehow "know" (in this inner space) that it is not about us, even when it seems to be directed specifically at us. And, further, we don't know how we arrived at this point of view, but we believe it anyway!

The second experience in this inner space is a growing tolerance of the poor choices we have made in our own lives. We have a new point of view that recognizes how really misinformed we have been. We "see" ourselves with much greater clarity, and we see how we bought into attitudes and patterns of behavior that hurt us and hurt others. We begin to see the action of the "false self" in our lives.

We learn that the spaciousness we have inside ourselves is also a place of remarkable creativity and peace. We come to trust this place as a spot of decision-making for those really complicated problems we find in our daily lives. Rather than immediately reacting to the events that trouble us, we find new resources for coping when we enter this space. For some of us it feels like our own "control room," where we find choices we might have missed otherwise.

We can enter this space free of any solutions to our predicament, with an attitude of patient waiting, and find alternatives that seem to fit our deeper selves. Over time, this oasis becomes a daily destination. Our prayer periods increasingly feel like a necessity for good health. If we miss a session, we recognize the loss of a chance for deep inner rest. We don't feel an obligation to do centering prayer, it has become integral in our daily lives for a feeling of well-being and clarity.

> When I started the practice of centering prayer I noticed I wasn't nervous. I saw that nothing was expected of me. I could figure this out at my own pace. All I had to do was be open-minded and see that there is no wrong way to connect myself with the Divine. . . . I can do it anytime, day or night, working or exercising. It brings me back to me.
> —C.N.

The Divine Therapy

We all want a vacation from ourselves. We want to get beyond the chatter, the noise, the constant inner commentary we tell ourselves. For most of us, the commentary is negative: that is, our reactions to the mini-events in our lives seem to remind us that we are not good enough, or did things the wrong way, or screwed up again in some fashion. That's one of the reasons why we watch TV, put on headphones, and try to lose ourselves in any number of distractions. We want to get away from ourselves.

This is not a new experience for us. We see that this need to get far away is the origin of many poor choices and bad decisions. As we sit in our cells we can feel the poison of discouragement slowly invade the vital organs of our lives. It invades our centering prayer practice as well: *Why am I doing this? I'm not getting anything out of this. I'm still angry.*

Yet still on some days when we sit in our prayer group circle we hear the whisper of hope: *What do I have to lose? Where else can I go, really, to turn around the downward spiral of my life?*

We find new appreciation for contemplative prayer as a prayer without words because our pain and discouragement is greater than any imagined advice or instruction.

As we hold still we begin our own private therapy session with the One we are waiting for, the One who knows us through and through. These meetings at our inner core are the medicine for the poison that is debilitating our spirit.

We know that centering prayer is not the simple, easy road to bliss. It takes courage to face the pains and struggles of a lifetime. When we enter this personal space, all the false notions of ourselves are there to welcome us! All the false promises of our addictive behavior and our phony thinking are waiting for us. We come to understand that we can only change the way we see things by dealing directly with our pain and confusion. We find that facing this pain in centering prayer removes some of its sting.

After a time, we notice that an almost imperceptible change enters our lives. We are less fearful of the pain. We see that by neither resisting the pain nor holding onto it, it starts to fade. Moments of relief emerge. We find that we can grasp the part we play in our own downward spiral. These "therapy sessions" empower our recovery. The transformation we crave is at hand.

Practitioners of centering prayer call this "divine therapy" for a specific reason. The Spirit alive in us seems to know the exact material deeply buried in our unconscious to bring into our awareness. Those long-forgotten hurts we experienced as a little person can now come back to us as an adult for our consideration and compassion.

Who better to be with when you remember the pain of being left behind? We can give ourselves now exactly what we needed then. With God's help we become our best therapist, as we sit silently in the awareness of this experience of long ago.

The best thing about the practice of centering prayer is my time alone with God.—**Aaron Jones**

Religion is largely populated by people afraid of hell; spirituality begins to make sense to those who have been through hell—that is, who have drunk deeply of life's difficulties.—**Richard Rohr**, *Things Hidden*, p. 100

Africa: Osun Procession by Betty La Duke

Lord, you search me and you know me, you know when I sit and stand, you understand my thoughts from afar. My journey and my rest you mark. You know all my ways. Even before a word is on my tongue, Lord, you know it all. You formed my inmost being, you knit me in my mother's womb, my very self you knew!—**Psalm 139** (adapted)

A Mother Notices the Change

At each visit, too numerous now to count, I would search for glimpses of the quiet and introspective person he was, but prison life had shoved it way back down inside. Most often, I would see a haunted look in his face, a slump to his shoulders, a lack of animation, a dullness in his eyes, and a beaten-down demeanor. An overall general disconnect. All I could do was silently pray to God for something to bring him back to himself, for a light at the end of the tunnel.

Then, in the summer of 2012, I noticed a dramatic change. I got an excited phone call from him telling me about a class he had begun to attend at the prison. It dealt with centering prayer. This was what he needed, and an answer to my prayers.

In the last two years, his demeanor has changed markedly. He has things to say now, excitedly, and he reaches out to other inmates in the Visiting Room, something he never did. He is developing insight and compassion, two valuable things the prison system can take from you. He is still quiet and introspective, but he walks lighter now; some of the weight of prison life is gone. And wonderful laughter has returned.

Because of this involvement in the centering prayer program at Folsom Prison, his world has gotten larger and is no longer so confining. He has found a source of freedom, right here in the midst of a well-controlled prison. And that light at the end of the tunnel is now the light I see in his eyes!

—Robin Gilmore
March 2014

Jesus is not changing his Father's mind about us; he is changing our mind about what is real and what is not.—**Richard Rohr**, *Things Hidden*, p. 189

The Gospel truths invite a degree of trust in God that seems impossible in the so-called real world. And they require the most awful and awesome spiritual sacrifice: letting-go of control.—**Gerald May**, *The Propaganda of Willfulness*

Part 3

A Contemplative View of the Gospels

After the writing of the gospels, the early Church would gather together to hear the Word of God. This was not simply because most people could not read. They heard the Word together because they found a method of hearing the gospels that brought the text to life. One would read a certain text, pause in silence, then slowly read the text again. It would sink into their memory and imagination. ("I am the good shepherd.") In the context of prayer and openness to the Word they would sit and let the text marinate through them.

They would sit in silence and let the text take them to the place they needed to go. Because they were familiar with silence, and contemplation was a familiar form of prayer, they could "rest in God" as the text worked them. Since they were engaging their memory and imagination, they would bypass a strict rational analysis of the text. For these listeners, the text had more than one meaning. How the text opened them was the goal.

Through this practice, called *lectio divina* (sacred reading), the gospels invite us to a degree of trust in God that seems impossible in today's so-called real world. As this process flows in us we find that gospel truths are much more about *metanoia* (a Greek word the gospel writers used, usually translated as *repent*, that actually means changing our view of the way God works in the world) than about commandments and laws of behavior. These gospel truths lead us to the great spiritual sacrifice: letting go of control and putting our lives into the hands of God.

The following passages prompt us to take another view of the wisdom sayings of Jesus. We begin to notice more clearly Jesus' own contemplative practice of "resting in God" when he prayed. His prayer relationship well summarizes the source of both his wisdom and ours.

The Contemplative Jesus: Model for Meditation

It took the early Church nearly three hundred years to define and write an acceptable explanation of the divine and human Jesus. Their formula leaves a lot out, as it simply states that Jesus was fully human and fully divine. His divinity was the same as the divinity of the Father. His humanity was like ours except he was without sin. His divinity did not substitute for his humanity, and his humanity did not take the place of his divinity. Rather, Jesus modeled for us how to be fully human, and as such how to become divine.

With this as background, his prayer practice takes on new light. As a human person he had to find his human identity (*Who am I?*) and figure out how his identity related to God (*Who is God?*) the way we all do, by trusting his inner experience of the Divine and by study and conversation. As we read scripture for hints of this "experience of the Divine," we find Jesus spent long periods of prayer "throughout the night." Although he taught his disciples the "Our Father" as the necessary way to approach the Mystery he called *Father*, there can be no doubt that he would not spend those long nights in prayer simply repeating the "Our Father" over and over again—it wouldn't be human.

If he was truly "human" (like us)—encountering the demonic, healing the pain of the sorrowful, and trying to get through to his religious leaders of the day, as he did— then he must have needed that time of night to sort out his relationship with the Ultimate Mystery: *Who am I? Who is God?* and *Who am I in relation to God?* must have been the core pursuit of his life.

Are our lives any different? Our core questions in figuring out the central meaning of our existence are the same. Isn't this the central theme of our contemplative practice? Could it be any different for him? Jesus found his answers in contemplation. Can it be any different for us?

We find the faith *of* Jesus is as important as faith *in* Jesus.

A Nobody Announces a Somebody

The beginning of the gospel of Jesus Christ, the Son of God. As it is written in Isaiah the prophet:

> Behold, I send my messenger ahead of you,
>   who will prepare your way;
> the voice of one crying in the wilderness,
>   "make ready the way of the lord,
>   make his paths straight."

John the Baptist appeared in the wilderness preaching a baptism of repentance for the forgiveness of sins. And all the country of Judea was going out to him, and all the people of Jerusalem; and they were being baptized by him in the Jordan River, confessing their sins. John was clothed with camel's hair and wore a leather belt around his waist, and his diet was locusts and wild honey. And he was preaching, and saying, "After me One is coming who is mightier than I, and I am not fit to stoop down and untie the thong of His sandals. I baptized you with water; but He will baptize you with the Holy Spirit."
—Mark 1:1–8

The writers of the four gospels had a real problem on their hands: how to start writing about Jesus and to prepare their readers for the deep realities of his life.

All four of the gospels use a dramatic character to announce the coming of Jesus. He is like an announcer who comes out before a play and prepares you for the drama that is about to unfold. Even the two gospel writers (Matthew and Luke) who start their gospels by describing Jesus' birth and the miraculous events surrounding it, eventually get to this "announcer" when they describe the adult life of Jesus.

Who was he? John the Baptist. He was neither a priest, nor a religious authority, nor a member of the temple. He apparently had neither earthly power nor position, neither wealth nor influential family background. He had no special education and wasn't living in the center of a dominant culture. In short, he was a nobody: an odd person for God to choose to announce the coming of his son, our savior and liberator.

Well, then, what did he have to say? Again, oddly, his words are strangely confusing for the setting. The writers tell us he came as a "witness" to "testify" on behalf of Jesus. *Witness* and *testify* are legal terms, as we well know, used in court to prove or deny one's innocence. Is Jesus already accused? Of what? What is going on here? Can this John be a credible witness if he had no power and religious authority? How do we know? Would you believe him?

Yet, without any official authority from the temple officials, the recognized religious leaders of the time, John performed the deeply religious ritual of baptism and exhorted his followers to "repentance for the forgiveness of sins." Probably just like his listeners at the time and down through the centuries we have grossly misunderstood the core meaning of this "repentance for the forgiveness of sins."

This "repentance" is less about guilt and shame for our mistakes and bad decisions and more the root notion of a change of heart, or a change in the way we see life and live life. John is saying, *Start looking with different eyes; open your life to an entirely different way of living. Leave behind the many ways we dissipate and narcotize the divine energy that comes to us. Be willing to change the habits and character flaws that prevent the Divine breaking into our lives. Change the way you behave; be prepared for a radically new way of relating to God and each other.*

Now this is starting to make sense in light of John as the forerunner of Jesus. Knowing what is to come, and the profound words and actions of Jesus, we need a new way of looking at life to be able to comprehend the enormity of the invitation coming to us in the person of Jesus. The Jesus that John is announcing is not another "nice" religious person, irrelevant to our deepest fears and most personal conflicts. On the contrary, John is preparing us for a reality we can easily dismiss and not even see, if we use our normal habitual way of living life.

John is saying that this is no ordinary prophet coming to Israel, like so many others who have guided them in the past. No, this is the One. This is the One to bring us into the depths of relationship with the Divine, a depth so intimate and complete that with him we can call God *Father* and God can call us *Son*.

How would you announce his coming?

The Initiation of Jesus

And he was preaching, and saying, "After me One is coming who is mightier than I, and I am not fit to stoop down and untie the thong of His sandals. I baptized you with water; but He will baptize you with the Holy Spirit." In those days Jesus came from Nazareth in Galilee and was baptized by John in the Jordan. Immediately coming up out of the water, He saw the heavens opening, and the Spirit like a dove descending upon Him; and a voice came out of the heavens: "You are My beloved Son, in You I am well-pleased."
—Mark 1:7–11

The Gospel of Mark is an in-your-face, fast-paced narrative of the life and death of Jesus. The beginning of the story in the opening chapter describes Jesus' encounter with John the Baptist. Jesus approaches John without fanfare, presenting himself simply as one needing baptism. Remember, John the Baptist was preaching to large crowds around Jerusalem. He urged repentance and conversion. He demanded a change of heart and mind to be ready for the coming of the Holy One. John spoke as a messenger to prepare the way for Jesus, of whom John said he was not worthy to fasten his sandals.

This opening story illustrates a deep confusion surrounding the identity of Jesus. Why, if Jesus is the One, would he be presenting himself to John to be baptized?

Baptism then, as now, is a deep and significant initiation into a new way of thinking, leaving one's old life behind, and committing to a new way of living. If Jesus was fully human and fully divine, as we have come to believe, why did he ask for baptism?

One tradition in the Church answers the question by pointing to the words that Jesus heard after his baptism: "You are my beloved Son; with you I am well-pleased." This tradition says that Jesus is the Son of God. This revelation invites us to follow Jesus because he is God's Son.

But another tradition looks at this story and wonders what Jesus must be experiencing to even approach John for baptism. As a human being, Jesus' own inner experience prompts him to reach out to John. Apparently, like the others seeking John's baptism, Jesus wants this "change of heart and mind." Apparently, he is looking for a way out of his sense of separation and disconnection. He must feel an inner draw to God. As a person, he probably is feeling the need to be identified with something or someone greater than himself. For Jesus, this is the inner movement of initiation we call baptism.

Whatever Jesus' inner motives, it is clear that his life was radically changed when he emerged from the water. He could not go back. Jesus had to go into the desert to begin to assimilate the new experience. His baptism was a major event that influenced the course of his life. He now responds in ever-deeper ways to the invitations of the Divine.

It is no different for us. The dramatic events in Jesus' life are reflected in our own. We experience from time to time a sense of disconnection and separation from others, as if there is some design defect in us. We, too, experience an inexpressible longing for wholeness and healing, a need to go out of ourselves. At least a part of us is drawn in the same way as Jesus was drawn to baptism by John. Our invitation is one and the same as Jesus' invitation into the life of God.

Like Jesus, the experience of deep initiation begins to address our deeper longings, and profoundly changes the course of our lives. Take a close look. We are not making this up. We are responding to a deep, inner need for wholeness. The holy ones tell us that God gives us the desires he intends to fulfill in us. Listen closely and hear the words spoken to Jesus, the same words now spoken to us: "You are my beloved Son; with you I am well-pleased."

Night Terror

When evening came, his disciples went down to the sea, got into a boat, and started across the sea to Capernaum. It was now dark, and Jesus had not yet come to them. The sea became rough because a strong wind was blowing. When they had rowed about three or four miles, they saw Jesus walking on the sea and coming near the boat, and they were terrified. But he said to them, "It is I; do not be afraid." Then they wanted to take him into the boat, and immediately the boat reached the land toward which they were going.
—**John 6:16–21** (English Standard Version)

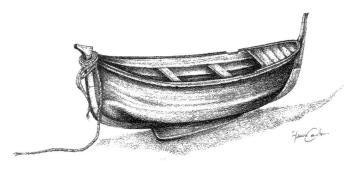

Prisoners are drawn to this story because it captures for them the heart of the journey of contemplative prayer. They identify with the disciples who are terrified and plead with Jesus to get into the boat to save them. He doesn't. Yet the boat suddenly and immediately gets the disciples to the other side. The story summarizes in perfect symbolic form the experience of centering prayer. Amid the darkness and the terror of a true encounter with the Divine our boat gets us to the other side.

Why does this story have such an impact on prisoners? Experts tell us that real change, personal transformation, comes only in nonordinary experience. Somehow, when we break the trance-like consciousness of our day-to-day living we can move into a spaciousness that invites real change. We don't know how this change happens, it just does. We also know that centering prayer is a continuing nonordinary experience. It's the boat that takes us to the other shore.

When our nonordinary experience involves encounters with the Divine, we realize a fuller integration of our deepest desires. In centering prayer practice, we discover our yearning to reach the "other shore" of our desire to be the person God created us to be. We recognize that our momentum is carrying us to be that person. We just don't know how to do it. Like the disciples in the boat, we can't get to the other side by ourselves.

By sitting as we do in prayer we find that our simple presence to the Divine, even in fear and trembling, brings a new level of wholeness into our lives. We hear, "It is I; do not be afraid," and trust our true self will take us the rest of the way.

The Parable of the Prodigal Son

Then Jesus said, "There was a man who had two sons. The younger of them said to his father, 'Father, give me the share of the property that will belong to me.' So he divided his property between them. A few days later the younger son gathered all he had and traveled to a distant country, and there he squandered his property in dissolute living. When he had spent everything, a severe famine took place throughout that country, and he began to be in need. So he went and hired himself out to one of the citizens of that country, who sent him to his fields to feed the pigs. He would gladly have filled himself with the pods that the pigs were eating; and no one gave him anything. But when he came to himself he said, 'How many of my father's hired hands have bread enough and to spare, but here I am dying here of hunger! I will get up and go to my father, and I will say to him, "Father, I have sinned against heaven, and before you in your sight; I am no longer worthy to be called your son; treat make me like as one of your hired hands."' So he set off got up and went to his father. But while he was still far off, his father saw him and was filled with compassion; and he ran and put his arms around him and kissed him. Then the son said to him, 'Father, I have sinned against heaven and before you; I am no longer worthy to be called your son.' But the father said to his slaves, 'Quickly, bring out a robe—the best one—and put it on him; put a ring on his finger and sandals on his feet. And get the fatted calf and kill it, and let us eat and celebrate; for this son of mine was dead and is alive again; he was lost and is found!' And they began to celebrate.

"Now his elder son was in the field; and when he came and approached the house, he heard music and dancing. He called one of the slaves and asked what was going on. He replied, 'Your brother has come, and your father has killed the

fatted calf, because he has got him back safe and sound.' Then he became angry and refused to go in. His father came out and began to plead with him. But he answered his father, 'Listen! For all these years I have been working like a slave for you, and I have never disobeyed your command; yet you have never given me even a young goat so that I might celebrate with my friends. But when this son of yours came back, who has devoured your property with prostitutes, you killed the fatted calf for him!' Then the father said to him 'Son, you are always with me, and all that is mine is yours. But we had to celebrate and rejoice, because this brother of yours was dead and has come to life; he was lost and has been found.'"—**Luke 15:11–32** (New Revised Standard Version)

The story of the prodigal or lost son is a parable, a technique Jesus used a lot to shock his listeners into the essence of the point he wanted to make.

Although the story is usually named after the younger son who leaves the fold before his time, the star of the parable is the father. His extraordinary actions are the real focus of the story.

Some prisoners think that neither the younger nor the elder son actually loved their father. The younger returned home because he was simply fed up with his rotten lot, and figured in his dire need that he'd be better off as a slave at his father's house. The elder son displayed a similar selfishness. His jealousy at the return of his younger brother brought out the worst in him. Neither brother loved the father: the first broke all the rules, and that didn't work for him. The elder kept all the rules and, as it turns out, that didn't work very well for him either.

We can usually see a part of ourselves in the younger brother, particularly in our early years. As we get older we "come to our senses" and realize that there must be a better way of living our lives. Life sentences have a way of showing us that our plans are not working. The elder-brother part of ourselves is less obvious. After all, isn't life about keeping the rules? Can we keep all the rules and still be selfish and self-centered?

It's the attitude and actions of the father in the parable that come center stage for our consideration. Jesus' listeners would have been shocked at the actions of the father. Men of wealth and stature, as is clear from this story, never left their palace to greet anyone. Here, the father was out of his house, and seeing his son from a distance he ran to him! Imagine a head of a huge household leaving his house, and waiting and watching for the return of a son who prematurely took his inheritance, squandered it, and sheepishly is returning home, wondering if he'll be accepted as a slave. This would be shocking to those listening to this parable.

Before the son can even get out "make me one of your slaves," the father has already set in motion the grand celebration reserved for the visit of royalty. No wonder the elder son, keeping all the rules, was furious. Where was his portion, his part of the inheritance? Once again, the father was well within acceptable boundaries to set this son straight. He didn't do it. He was so taken by the return of his lost son that nothing would stop the celebration.

This story comes in Chapter 15 of Luke, right after the story of the lost sheep and the lost coin. In each of these parables the central message is the joy of finding that which was lost. It's the father's joy that Jesus is trying to demonstrate, not the need for the repentance of the younger son nor the need for generosity from the elder. Jesus is trying to tell us that this is who the Father is: he wants us with him because that is who he is; he can't be indifferent. This is the Father we encounter in our Silence; this is the Divine Mystery that loves us, no matter what.

A Prisoner's Reflection on the Prodigal Son

I think I know why the prodigal son cashed out his inheritance. He couldn't take it anymore! The older brother says he stayed home out of a loving devotion to the father, but I don't buy it. I think he stayed because he's scared of the consequences of disobedience.

Is love about obedience? Is it fear of the consequence of not following the rules? Something's not quite right here. So, not able to understand this, like the younger son in the story, I decided to go it alone. My way of cashing out was to terrorize, brutalize, and make others come face to face with the world "they" had created for me. Yet, somewhere beneath all this mayhem was a voice. It terrified me. I did everything not to listen to it. Yet that damn voice wouldn't leave me.

Like the prodigal son, it hit me: I'm all alone and I'm scared! Maybe my brother followed the rules out of fear. But I realized that I'm scared, too! Terrified. Fear is woven into the fabric of my DNA. I spent so much time passing judgment, heaping condemnation, brutalizing others in an attempt to shatter their "false idols," I never realized their world is my world too, and I'm destroying it. Destroying my own world, destroying myself. Those who placed burdens upon me did it because they were and are also afraid. Like me, they just didn't know how to ask for help.

I learned that the voice that terrified me is the one that doesn't give up on me, even when I want to, like the father in the story. This voice reminds us that we are better than we feel ourselves to be. It's time for me to start my journey back home. I wonder if they'll receive me after all these years?

A Most Threatening Proposal

For the kingdom of heaven is just like a man about to go on a journey, who called his own slaves and entrusted his possessions to them.

To one he gave five talents, to another, two, and to another, one, each according to his own ability; and he went on his journey. Immediately the one who had received the five talents went and traded with them, and gained five more talents. In the same manner the one who had received the two talents gained two more. But he who received the one talent went away, and dug a hole in the ground and hid his master's money.

Now after a long time the master of those slaves came and settled accounts with them. The one who had received the five talents came up and brought five more talents, saying, "Master, you entrusted five talents to me. See, I have gained five more talents." His master said to him, "Well done, good and faithful slave. You were faithful with a few things, I will put you in charge of many things; enter into the joy of your master."

Also the one who had received the two talents came up and said, "Master, you entrusted two talents to me. See, I have gained two more talents." His master said to him, "Well done, good and faithful slave. You were faithful with a few things, I will put you in charge of many things; enter into the joy of your master."

And the one also who had received the one talent came up and said, "Master, I knew you to be a hard man, reaping where you did not sow and gathering where you scattered no seed. And I was afraid, and went away and hid your talent in the ground. See, you have what is yours."

But his master answered and said to him, "You wicked, lazy slave, you knew that I reap where I did not sow and gather where I scattered no seed. Then you ought to have put my money in the bank, and on my arrival I would have received my money back with interest. Therefore take away the talent from him, and give it to the one who has the ten talents."

For to everyone who has, more shall be given, and he will have an abundance; but from the one who does not have, even what he does have shall be taken away. Throw out the worthless slave into the outer darkness; in that place there will be weeping and gnashing of teeth.—**Matthew 25:14–30**

As a good teacher summarizes his teaching, Matthew's gospel in Chapter 25 gives us a final summary of Jesus' teaching.

Not surprisingly, Jesus uses a parable to teach clearly what he is all about. Parables emphasize and grab our attention away from the normal way we think of ourselves and our lives. In Jesus' time, his parables shocked his listeners into a whole new way of thinking about deep and important life themes. These parables of Jesus had an extra teaching bonus: they showed how Jesus' own life was consistent with the radical teachings of the parable stories.

This parable of the "talents" is no less radical and shocking than the others. What appears to be an unjust punishment of one servant is an accurate description of the outcomes of fundamental choices in our lives. To appreciate this outcome, realize that the word *talents* in the parable, literally meaning "coins of value," really means something of great personal value. Jesus' listeners would understand that he was referring to their long-held religious traditions and beliefs.

In particular, when Jesus referred to the "talents entrusted to the servants" he was describing entrusting to his disciples all his life teaching—his total human experience—about the Father, living in union with the Father, and living a life of selfless loving with one another. Jesus' "possessions" were nothing other than the totality of all he lived and taught before he was arrested and executed.

From this perspective it is easier to see how the two servants who did something with their master's "possessions" (v. 14) were actually then doing something with the entirety of Jesus' experience and teachings. They, of course, would be rewarded for their risk-taking with double their initial gift, greater responsibilities, and their "master's joy." In other words, by taking the risk and incorporating Jesus' teaching and living as he did, they would experience themselves the depth of the joy experienced by Jesus. By giving love and kindness they would find themselves with ever-greater depths of love and kindness.

The opposite is true for the one who in fear of this master buried his initial possessions. "Buried" means he did not accept the invitation and take the risk of living his experience of Jesus. He was unable to overcome his fear of changing his habitual way of acting and thinking. He couldn't leave his routine to respond to the invitation of Christ. His one talent was taken from him, not in punishment, but because this is what naturally happens when fear controls our lives. The parable wants us to observe paralysis of fear to encourage us to take the risk to push fear into the background.

"For to everyone who has, more shall be given, and he will have an abundance; but from the one who does not have, even what he does have shall be taken away" (v. 29). This is the "shock" of the parable. This seemingly unjust conclusion, however, is not unjust at all. It describes perfectly the reality of following the life and teaching of the Master Himself.

The Decontamination of the Temple

The Passover of the Jews was near, and Jesus went up to Jerusalem. And He found in the temple those who were selling oxen and sheep and doves, and the money changers seated at their tables. And He made a scourge of cords, and drove them all out of the temple, with the sheep and the oxen; and He poured out the coins of the money changers and overturned their tables; and to those who were selling the doves, He said, "Take these things away; stop making My Father's house a place of business." His disciples remembered that it was written, "zeal for your house will consume me." The Jews then said to Him, "What sign do You show us as your authority for doing these things?" Jesus answered them, "Destroy this temple, and in three days I will raise it up." The Jews then said, "It took forty-six years to build this temple, and will You raise it up in three days?" But He was speaking of the temple of His body. So when He was raised from the dead, His disciples remembered that He said this; and they believed the Scripture and the word which Jesus had spoken.
—John 2:13–22

Occasionally, Jesus' behavior is so unpredictable and apparently violent we can wonder who this person is. Such is the case with the above reading, traditionally known as "The Cleansing of the Temple." This cleansing is so deep and thorough we should describe it as a "decontamination"—a clearing out of life-threatening, toxic materials.

It is important to note that this reading is from the fourth gospel, the Gospel of John, and it is radically different from the first three gospels in its portrayal of who this person Jesus is. The Jesus of Matthew, Mark, and Luke is the wisdom Jesus, whose insight and intimacy with the Ultimate Mystery (God) is so close that Jesus calls God *Father*. With the fourth gospel, Jesus goes beyond this intimate relationship to claim that he and the Father are one and the same. What can we make of this? Can we possibly believe the claims of Jesus in this gospel?

John's gospel story gives us valuable clues to understand the depth of the mystery Jesus is laying out to us.

Remember, the temple was the central place of worship for the Jewish people. An entire cult of worship had developed around their worshiping practices. It was based on the assumption that the vast majority of people were sinners—that is "unclean"—and needed temple worship to be cleansed. The religious cult obligated them to make amends through sacrifices of sheep, oxen, and (for the really poor) doves (pigeons) for their unclean status. Conveniently, the authorities made the rules, sold the animals for sacrifice, and mediated their connection with God.

This sacrificial cult, the people thought, was the only way they could come to God. At root, the religious authorities persuaded the people that their relationship with God could only be mediated by the authority's permission. If the poor and excluded didn't follow the rules, they were not "justified" or in right relationship with their God. The rules were extensive and governed everything from eating to praying to worshiping. All freedom of personal intimacy with God was removed.

It is this attitude and belief in the impossibility of approaching God directly that is at the root of Jesus throwing out the merchants and bankers from the temple. He is not simply driving out the merchants and religious authorities; he is redefining at the deepest level how we can approach the Divine. It is not some clarifying of an essentially helpful religious practice; it is a totally different perspective on how to live in union with God. This driving out of the temple authorities was nothing other than a redefining of the entire temple ideology, the core of Jewish religious practice—a through toxic decontamination.

Jesus' total rejection of the authority's teaching on how to enter into right relationship with God prompts them to ask: *Where is your authority to be doing and saying this?* Jesus' "destroy this temple and in three days I will raise it up" confuses them even more, as they say that it took forty-six years to build the temple. But it gives us a final clue to his meaning and motive.

The gospel writer is telling us, with Jesus' words, that from now on the Jerusalem temple, which has been turned into a marketplace, has been replaced by the risen body of Jesus as the true holy place. As with the experience described of Jesus, we may encounter the Divine, first and foremost, in the depth of our own hearts, in the awareness of the Transcendent One dwelling within us.

This is good news for us. Following the risen Christ, we Christians know that we can go directly to intimacy with God in our deepest selves. We come together in the body of Christ to share in the Body of Christ. As Jesus and the Father are one, we too, through our union with Christ, become one with the Father as well.

The purpose of contemplation is neither to improve our morals or ethics nor to perfect our personality to win friends and influence people, nor any kind of self-improvement or self-aggrandizing goal. The "purpose" of contemplation is to lose our self: "He who saves his life loses it, while he who loses his life for my sake discovers who he really is."

—**Gregory Mayers**, *Listen to the Desert*, p. 41

After Our Death: What Can We Expect?

All that the Father gives Me will come to Me, and the one who comes to Me I will certainly not cast out. For I have come down from heaven, not to do My own will, but the will of Him who sent Me. This is the will of Him who sent Me, that of all that He has given Me I lose nothing, but raise it up on the last day. For this is the will of My Father, that everyone who beholds the Son and believes in Him will have eternal life, and I Myself will raise him up on the last day."
—John 6:37–40

No matter the religious or cultural perspective, death— that of our loved ones and ours—is the topic we avoid most of the time. Let's not avoid it here. Let's find what meaning it has in our lives.

John 6:37–40 is one of the most complicated passages of the fourth gospel and offers a helpful perspective. Remember this fourth gospel is like no other gospel, written by someone in a community that was formed around someone who knew Jesus personally. This gospel describes a Jesus who comes talking about "eternal life," coming from the Father and going back to the Father, and taking us with him. He seems to have a lot to say about death.

In the chapters preceding this passage, the religious authorities of the time find Jesus to be different from the religious leader they were expecting. The Jewish leaders wanted a political leader; Jesus preached nonviolent love. In fact, Jesus did not seem to go along with many of their religious doctrines or rules for religious observance. So they were constantly asking for a "sign," or proof, that he was the real thing. He gave them a sign, but not the one they wanted. The more he talked, the more confused they became: *Who is this person? Where did he come from? What sign does he need to give us?*

They ask him for a sign comparable to the manna (bread) given to their ancestors in the desert by Moses. Jesus follows up on the request by telling them that there is in fact a "new manna" given by the Father, and that "new manna" is himself! This new manna will give life to the world. This new manna, this bread of life that gives life to the world, is God's revelation of Jesus. It is God's nourishing Word, when accepted and lived, that becomes the source of life.

So Jesus continues: "Everyone who sees the Son and believes in him may have eternal life, and I shall raise him up on the last day."

Accepting the revelation of Jesus as the full embodiment of God's unconditional love for each one of us is the core of all Christianity. It is the best "sign" we receive. By accepting this revelation, living a life of unselfish love, we are told that we will not die, just as Jesus did not die, but we will be raised up, just as Jesus was raised up, by the Father: *Can I believe this? Is this passage credible with my own experience such that it gives me hope for overcoming my death and the death of my loved ones?*

We must ultimately ask ourselves: *Is Jesus credible? Is his message true? Could Jesus actually be the person that is*

God's Son? What theology and creeds tell us is one thing. Our experience of the Divine in contemplative prayer, just as Jesus' experience of the "Father" in his Contemplation Prayer, gives us a whole new level of understanding of our ultimate destiny. We can, like Jesus, come to accept our experience as a promise of life without end.

To Whom Am I Indebted?

Then the Pharisees went and plotted together how they might trap him in what He said. And they sent their disciples to him, along with the Herodians, saying, "Teacher, we know that You are truthful and teach the way of God in truth, and defer to no one; for You are not partial to any. Tell us then, what do You think? Is it lawful to give a poll-tax to Caesar, or not?" But Jesus perceived their malice, and said, "Why are you testing me, you hypocrites? Show me the coin used for the poll-tax." And they brought him a denarius. And He said to them, "Whose likeness and inscription is this?" They said to him, "Caesar's." Then He said to them, "Then render to Caesar the things that are Caesar's; and to God the things that are God's." And hearing this, they were amazed, and leaving Him, they went away.—**Matthew 22:15–22**

Jesus is heading into his final days. He is now in Jerusalem, the center of religious practice, preaching in the temple, the holiest place for the religious people of his time. In a few days he will be arrested, convicted, and executed.

He speaks of God, the Ultimate Mystery, in a way like no other. He calls God his "Father," and tells the poor and marginalized (the "unclean") that God is their Father as well: they are full heirs and participants in the Kingdom he describes. Moreover, he criticizes the religious authorities for their hypocrisy and deceit, for using their authority in ways that misguide their followers. For this, the religious leaders want to discredit him before his followers and entrap him in a violation against the Roman authorities.

So a delegation of religious leaders sets a trap. They would use the tax law and Roman coins. (A Roman coin had the inscription "August, Son of God" in tribute to Augustus Caesar, the Emperor of Rome. For any good Jew, it would be idolatry to use this coin, and a sin against their God.) So they approach Jesus, and after flattering him, ask him, "Is it lawful to pay the census tax to Caesar or not?" They knew that if Jesus said "yes" he would be considered a collaborator with the Roman authorities, and be despised by the devout religious Jews. If he said "no," he would be considered subversive, subject to arrest by the Romans.

After holding the coin, Jesus said: "Repay to Caesar what belongs to Caesar, and to God what belongs to God." He sidesteps the question, and raises a still more serious challenge to his questioners and to us. In effect, he tells us to repay the one to whom you are most indebted! That is, repay your obligations to the one who is most important to you, the one from whom you get your most personal self-definition. For a good Jew at the time, this could only mean God, since the very core of their religious belief was that they were God's chosen people. They were silenced by his answer.

Before we are too quick to put down the religious authorities trying to trap Jesus, we all would do well to ask ourselves the same question: *Where is my allegiance; to whom am I indebted? How do I define my deepest self?*

Recently, a prisoner whose parole date was rejected by the governor just 48 hours before his release told me, "They have my body, but they don't have my mind or my spirit." He didn't define his deepest self as a prisoner.

How would we respond to Jesus' challenge? To whom am I most indebted? What defines my deepest self?

All things are possible with God.

Segregated No More

And a leper came to Jesus, beseeching Him and falling on his knees before Him, and saying, "If you are willing, you can make me clean." Moved with compassion, Jesus stretched out His hand and touched him, and said to him, "I am willing; be cleansed." Immediately the leprosy left him and he was cleansed. And He sternly warned him and immediately sent him away, and He said to him, "See that you say nothing to anyone; but go, show yourself to the priest and offer for your cleansing what Moses commanded, as a testimony to them." But he went out and began to proclaim it freely and to spread the news around, to such an extent that Jesus could no longer publicly enter a city, but stayed out in unpopulated areas; and they were coming to Him from everywhere.
—Mark 1:40–45

During Jesus' time, anyone with a skin disease would be considered a leper, automatically declared unclean, and set apart from their community. Any contact with a leper would render a person unclean as well. Lepers remained isolated and excluded from their community. Yet, with a simple human touch, Jesus heals the leper and restores him to his community.

Notice the leper came to Jesus and "begged" him for healing. This leper, alone and isolated from his family, had hit bottom, he could sink no further. Hearing about Jesus' wonderful healings he came to believe that Jesus could heal him as well. In a real sense, he had already turned his life over to Christ even before he met him. The leper knew that Christ could heal him and remove his uncleanness. He was ready for a fundamental life shift.

Jesus did not disappoint him. He touched him. Imagine! No one touched lepers. It was forbidden by the religious authorities of the day. Yet, this compassionate touch of Jesus both healed the leprosy and restored the man to his kinfolk. He was no longer unclean.

What part of our life needs such healing? As prisoners we know the pain of segregation from our community. We can imagine our own personal encounter with Christ, just as the leper in the gospel. We can imagine what we would say to Christ given the chance.

> Only one who is patient and does not drown out the frightening silence in which God dwells . . . can already hear with ease and already appreciate something of the eternal life that is already inwardly given to us. . . .—**Karl Rahner,** *The Great Church Year,* p. 10

Life in the Prison Wilderness

Immediately the Spirit impelled Him to go out into the wilderness. And He was in the wilderness forty days being tempted by Satan; and He was with the wild beasts, and the angels were ministering to Him.—**Mark 1:12–13**

Prison inmates understand what it means to live in the wilderness. It's a place that is stripped of life's routines and activities to the degree that only the raw necessities of life remain. In prison, as in the wilderness, people are subjected to powers greater than themselves. And subjected in a fashion that allows only submission to those powers greater than themselves.

Why in the world would Jesus be drawn to the desert? Remember, he had just received an extraordinary initiation by John the Baptist where he heard the words: "You are my beloved Son; with you I am well pleased." Why would the same Spirit draw him into the desert, a wilderness filled with danger and the threat of death?

Jesus' experience in the desert is another initiation into his mission as the Father's son. Instead of beginning his preaching immediately after his baptism, he begins his preaching after his desert experience. He learned something in the wilderness that he did not have after his baptism. Deprived of the usual conditions of life, he came upon the essentials of his life—those inner movements that defined exactly who he was at that time.

This is clearly the case for many prisoners. With the drudgery and routine, the near total inability to determine your physical conditions, what remains is the choice to evaluate your life at a different, more spiritual, level: the choice to live in the usual way, or to live in a fashion that is consistent with deeper realities of life.

Jesus came to see the outline and contours of his destiny: as one called by the Father to bring all men and women back to the Father on a deep and permanent level. This is a level that was threatening to the religious powers of his day, but one that is literally eternal for those that choose to follow him.

Prison can be such a place of initiation, as the desert was for Jesus. It can happen—if you step outside the usual way of thinking about your life. This is what Jesus meant by "repent." It is not simply about the confession of sin, but more importantly about a radically new way of viewing our lives. A contemplative lifestyle invites this new way of seeing our lives by allowing us to step outside the usual ways we consider our lives.

The Roofers

When He had come back to Capernaum several days afterward, it was heard that He was at home. And many were gathered together, so that there was no longer room, not even near the door; and He was speaking the word to them. And they came, bringing to Him a paralytic, carried by four men. Being unable to get to Him because of the crowd, they removed the roof above Him; and when they had dug an opening, they let down the pallet on which the paralytic was lying. And Jesus seeing their faith said to the paralytic, "Son, your sins are forgiven." But some of the scribes were sitting there and reasoning in their hearts, "Why does this man speak that way? He is blaspheming; who can forgive sins but God alone?"

Immediately Jesus, aware in His spirit that they were reasoning that way within themselves, said to them, "Why are you reasoning about these things in your hearts? Which is easier, to say to the paralytic, 'Your sins are forgiven'; or to say, 'Get up, and pick up your pallet and walk?' But so that you may know that the Son of Man has authority on earth to forgive sins" —He said to the *paralytic, "I say to you, get up, pick up your pallet and go home." And he got up and immediately picked up the pallet and went out in the sight of everyone, so that they were all amazed and were glorifying God, saying, "We have never seen anything like this."*—**Mark 2:1–12**

The men in the gospel passage clearly had strong feelings about their friend who was paralyzed. They knew the whole town was literally at Jesus' doorstep, so they found a creative way to get around the crowd and put their friend right in front of Jesus. They literally broke into the house through the roof in the hope of placing him in front of Jesus. Little did they know how profound this encounter with Jesus would be. Notice it is their love for their friend and their trust in Jesus that heal their friend. The text tells us that it is their faith that prompts Jesus to forgive his sin and remove his shame.

Details of the story say they were "unable to get near Jesus because of the crowd," so they break through the roof. Why are these fine points important?

"Breaking away from the crowd" and finding a unique approach to the Lord seem to go together. It goes on all the time in prison. It's not obvious and spectacular like the gospel story, but it is true and profound nonetheless. Someone is alone and suffering in their personal guilt, shame, and grief. Usually, they can't sleep. Sometimes the depth of their suffering is such that they can't eat or reach out to anyone. They are alone in their misery. The usual answers provided by "the crowd" the person hangs with—the hatred, resentment, and violence that control the crowd—no longer soothe the depth of their pain.

Then someone, maybe their "cellie" or some other observant individual, not part of the usual crowd, simply reaches out and points to a path through their nightmare. This is the way of the all-compassionate, forgiving Christ, described in the reading. These people know what the man is going through because they have been there themselves. They know also what Christ can do for him, because he has done it for them. They simply place him before Christ and he takes it from there.

The Incarceration of John the Baptist

This word about Jesus spread throughout Judea and all the surrounding country. The disciples of John the Baptist reported all these things to John. So John summoned two of his disciples and sent them to the Lord to ask, "Are you the one who is to come, or are we to wait for another?" When the men had come to him, they said, "John the Baptist has sent us to you to ask, 'Are you the one who is to come, or are we to wait for another?'" Jesus had just then cured many people of diseases, plagues, and evil spirits, and had given sight to many who were blind. And he answered them, "Go and tell John what you have seen and heard: the blind receive their sight, the lame walk, the lepers are cleansed, the deaf hear, the dead are raised, the poor have good news brought to them. And blessed is anyone who takes no offense at me."—**Luke 7:17–23**

John was in prison when he heard about the crowds flocking to Jesus (Mark 6:17). It doesn't take much thought for prisoners to understand what that must have been like for John. He starts to reevaluate his life: *What got me here in this prison? Will God take care of me?*

For all of his public life, John's primary message was one of reform and repent: "Change the way you think about Yahweh; understand that we have not been faithful to the Covenant, and we are about to pay the price for our breaking the sacred covenant." This is the message that Jesus heard when he consented to be baptized by John

(Mark 1:9). The power of John's baptism and the experience of God's presence for Jesus drove him out to the desert to try to take it all in. But when Jesus came back, he didn't resume his following of John. He chose to follow his own path.

Biblical scholars explain it this way: John believed in a return of a fiery prophet of reform, like Elijah, ushering in "the great and terrible day of the Lord" (Malachi 3:23). For John, Yahweh is coming to judge and condemn those not willing to repent. But Jesus' message and life were not at all of a condemnatory, threatening God. His experience of God, and therefore his message, described Yahweh as compassionate, tender, and merciful, with no desire to condemn or destroy or take revenge. Jesus' God comes to heal, set free, and make joyful. His most important example of Yahweh is the parable of the Prodigal Son.

This could not have been lost on the imprisoned John. Imagine his confusion and desperation. He had to be thinking something like his whole life—with all its austerity and hardship—was misdirected. How could he get it so wrong? Haven't we all, in our darker, alone moments, thought the same thing? *How could I have gotten it so wrong? So wrong that I'm sitting alone in a prison cell?* Some commentators suggest that his sending two of his disciples to Jesus (7:18 above) was for their sake. That is, John sent them because he wanted them to follow Jesus. But when we look at the entirety of John's message and preaching, and compare it with the message and preaching of Jesus, we find an entirely different, much more understandable reason he sent them—they were his emissaries to Jesus, asking him, *Did I get it wrong?*

Typically for Jesus, he doesn't put down John for not seeing things clearly. He simply tells John's followers, "The blind see, the lame walk, the lepers are cleansed, the deaf hear, the dead are raised, the poor have good news brought to them." In other words, Yahweh's presence among us is to heal, not judge, to offer compassion not punishment. By telling John what "they have seen and heard," the presence of God is unmistakable.

Maybe, as we hold still in our darker, alone moments, the same recognition will emerge.

An Invitation from Christ

Now after John had been taken into custody, Jesus came into Galilee, preaching the gospel of God, and saying, "The time is fulfilled, and the kingdom of God is at hand; repent and believe in the gospel."

As He was going along by the Sea of Galilee, He saw Simon and Andrew, the brother of Simon, casting a net in the sea; for they were fishermen. And Jesus said to them, "Follow Me, and I will make you become fishers of men."

Immediately they left their nets and followed Him. Going on a little farther, He saw James the son of Zebedee, and John his brother, who were also in the boat mending the nets. Immediately He called them; and they left their father Zebedee in the boat with the hired servants, and went away to follow Him.
—Mark 1:14–20

Mark's account of the beginning of Jesus' ministry shoots off like a rocket with Jesus taking over for the arrested John the Baptist, calling four new disciples, and then with their immediate decision to leave all and follow him. Somehow, this narrative seems to move too fast. We need more information on these all-important first encounters with Jesus—whom sometime later, not now, Peter would call "Christ."

Who could this person be in the flesh in order for Peter and the rest of them to literally drop their fishing nets and leave everything behind to follow him? This, of course, is of critical importance for us because we must deal with our own encounter with Christ, perhaps in a different form, but in an encounter nonetheless. What was it about this person who created this immediate reaction?

The gospels narrate several encounters of individuals with Christ. People followed him, asking him for all sorts of favors and healings. Many just wanted to hear him speak and hang around him. They apparently had no problem approaching him, questioning him, some after his arrest even hitting him in the face and belittling him. He hung out with the bottom rung of society, those who had little or no status or power—the kind of people who were called "unclean" in those days. In our day, we'd call them the "dregs of society." Yet Jesus had no problem at all confronting the powerful and the religious leaders of his time.

What would you expect to find if you were introduced to him, or he came walking by you doing your work at the prison? If he "saw" (verses 16, 19) you, he'd be directly interested in you; you'd have a sense that he knew the deepest, most hidden part of you. No doubt you'd have a sense that he wasn't judging you for your mistakes and dumb moves, and at the same time not hesitating to suggest a better way of thinking about life. You'd probably want to continue the conversation. Notice, Jesus would probably not tell you to love him. He wasn't about that.

Do you think you could meet him? That is, actually *meet* him directly? Would you want to? Our tradition tells us we can meet him in several ways.

We meet him in the gospels, those stories of people who had encounters with him. Reading these stories gives us a feel for who he is, since we know that the risen Jesus, Christ our Lord, in some mysterious way is the same human person people met those many years ago. We meet him by becoming aware that the Spirit can live inside of us by our awareness of our yearning for an encounter with him.

The Meaning of Life

Again the next day John was standing with two of his disciples, and he looked at Jesus as He walked, and said, "Behold, the Lamb of God!" The two disciples heard him speak, and they followed Jesus. And Jesus turned and saw them following, and said to them, "What do you seek?" They said to Him, "Rabbi (which translated means Teacher), where are You staying?" He said to them, "Come, and you will see." So they came and saw where He was staying; and they stayed with Him that day, for it was about the tenth hour. One of the two who heard John speak and followed Him, was Andrew, Simon Peter's brother. He found first his own brother Simon and said to him, "We have found the Messiah" (which translated means Christ). He brought him to Jesus. Jesus looked at him and said, "You are Simon the son of John; you shall be called Cephas" (which is translated Peter).—**John 1:35–42**

This passage is the beginning of the narrative of the life, death, and resurrection of Jesus according to John. The story is deceptively simple. John the Baptist is standing with two of his disciples, waiting and watching. Jesus makes his entrance onto the stage by walking along. John announces the arrival of "the Lamb," and the two disciples follow Jesus, at least to a distance wherein Jesus might notice that he is being followed. The question Jesus asks them is one he will ask others in various ways during the rest of the gospel: "What do you want?" Like most of us, the disciples seem intimidated by this apparently simple question. They respond by asking, "Teacher, where do you live?"

If we understood Greek we'd know that the disciples' simple question to Jesus was not: *Where do you live?* They were asking: *What is the meaning of your life? What is your life's purpose?* Suddenly, this question becomes a plea for help: *Where can we find the peace and happiness we need?* Isn't this the most important question in our own life? If we were there with the disciples, we'd ask Jesus the same question.

Jesus' short answer gives the key to discovering the meaning and purpose of our lives. He tells them, "Come and see." Jesus invites them to more than they are expecting. "You will find where I am staying in more ways than one." In today's language, Jesus is saying, "Come and hang out with me and you'll find your meaning and purpose in life."

Notice this is not some philosophical concept, nor some intellectual explanation of God's demands for us. Rather, Jesus invites them and us to walk with him and to learn from him, for only in this way will we discover the truth about God's love for us, and about our need to join Jesus in loving others. Nothing we can learn is more important than this.

I believe there is a moment for each of us when we come to realize that there must be more to life than we were led to believe. That there must be a meaning in life that is more than street smarts and worldly wisdom can offer. We see that our lives are truly "unmanageable" because we can't find the way to lasting peace and happiness by our schemes for success, power, and dominance.

From this deeply meaningful gospel episode, we learn two significant principles. First, the most important precondition for conversion to a new way of living is recognizing the profound inner yearning we have for wholeness and completion in our lives. And, second, the path toward wholeness and peace is the path of Jesus' invitation. Come and see selfless love in all his encounters and Selfless Love will come to us; in this encounter we will find the wholeness and peace of our heart's desire.

> The only true joy on earth is to escape from the prison of our own false self, and enter by love into union with the life who dwells and sings in the essence of every creature and in the core of our own souls.
> —**Thomas Merton**, *New Seeds of Contemplation*, p. 27

The One Important Truth

For God so loved the world, that He gave His only begotten Son, that whoever believes in Him shall not perish, but have eternal life. For God did not send the Son into the world to judge the world, but that the world might be saved through Him. He who believes in Him is not judged; he who does not believe has been judged already, because he has not believed in the name of the only begotten Son of God.—John 3:16–18

Several people who come to chapel, "lifers" who have been incarcerated for many years, have a special wisdom, gained through experience of living life in prison. This wisdom is not written in a book. It is a lived wisdom of the gut, a wisdom born of firsthand experience gained the hard way—through painful day-in day-out living.

The core of the wisdom comes from the credibility of the "lifer" himself. By his very life, one can tell that he lives the wisdom he is teaching. His words have power because his way of life works for him. So we call this wisdom "the truth." It is the one important piece of information that allows him to live in prison as a free man.

In the same way, this gospel focuses on the One Truth, the Only Important Truth, that Jesus is trying to teach his followers. It is the basic teaching of Jesus, repeated over and over again, in different ways, in different forms, in

Jesus' words and in his actions. The One Important Truth is this:

Jesus is God's Son
He has come into the world bringing God's own life
So that every person who believes him also has God's own life
And is now permanently accepted into God's inner life.

What then does it mean to "believe" Jesus? What does it mean to "believe" the lifer who has transformed his life? It is not having "faith" as we usually hear it. It is closer to trust. With the lifer, just hanging around him creates the trust. The same is true of Jesus: just hanging around him, watching him, listening to him creates the trust necessary to "believe" in him.

We tend to believe the transformed lifer because we recognize we don't know what we are doing. We don't know what truth about ourselves to believe. We end up believing in Jesus for many of the same reasons. Though we have no idea of the inner life of God, Jesus has the credibility to teach us. We can take the step to trust him. He'll take us the rest of the way.

The Mystery that Holds Us

From that time Jesus began to show His disciples that He must go to Jerusalem, and suffer many things from the elders and chief priests and scribes, and be killed, and be raised up on the third day. Peter took Him aside and began to rebuke Him, saying, "God forbid it, Lord! This shall never happen to You." But He turned and said to Peter, "Get behind Me, Satan! You are a stumbling block to Me; for you are not setting your mind on God's interests, but man's."—**Matthew 16:21–23**

Three times in Matthew's gospel Jesus has a dramatic confrontation with Peter. Each has its own specific meaning, and this passage's intense argument cuts into the deep notions of who Peter is and what this "Church" that Jesus says Peter will lead is all about.

There is no doubt that Jesus and Peter engaged, even triggered, each other. You may recall Jesus granted Peter's colossal, spontaneous request. Peter did indeed walk on water, just like the Lord himself, until he let his fear get the better of him. With this, Jesus, seemingly shaken himself, genuinely asks Peter, *Why didn't you trust me?*

In another face-to-face encounter, Peter responds eloquently to Jesus' question of "Who do you say that I am?" with the famous: "You are the Anointed One, the Son of God." Peter's unashamed declaration is met by Jesus' own declaration of Peter being the foundation of Jesus' "Church." This moment of triumphant mutual declaration is enshrined in Christian holy places throughout the world. Far fewer holy places throughout the world enshrine the words of this passage.

In this gospel passage, we hear that this "Anointed One" must soon suffer terribly, be humiliated and mocked by his own clan, tortured, and executed. And perhaps worse, the one whom Jesus thought knew him so well, the one Jesus relies on to lead Jesus' followers, he himself simply cannot, and will not, accept this outcome! So Jesus tells him off.

What did Peter not understand that led to this condemnation? Tradition answers: the Messiah was not to be leader of a human kingdom, but a divine kingdom established by the Father. But how did Peter miss this fundamental point when getting it so right only moments before?

Perhaps Peter was the first to make the mistakes we all make, the mistake that the Church, like its first leader, has made down through the centuries: we continue to interpret the life of Christ from the perspective of the educated, clergy class, rather than from the perspective of the marginalized, poor, and the oppressed. In the gospels, it's the lame, the blind, the prostitutes, the drunkards, the tax collectors, the sinners, the outsiders, and the foreigners who tend to follow Jesus.

When Jesus spoke about Peter leading his "Church," he was not referring to the hierarchical institution we frequently invoke for this saying. After all, the hierarchical institution of Jesus' own religion at the time was his fiercest enemy. Jesus meant something different. The root meaning of *Church* is something much deeper and more personal. It is the group that holds the Mystery together. Losing sight of the Mystery of Christ throwing his lot with the lowest of the low, we lose sight of who Jesus really is, and what his Church is all about.

Us versus Them

Jesus went away from there, and withdrew into the district of Tyre and Sidon. And a Canaanite woman from that region came out and began to cry out, saying, "Have mercy on me, Lord, Son of David; my daughter is cruelly demon-possessed." But He did not answer her a word. And His disciples came and implored Him, saying, "Send her away, because she keeps shouting at us." But He answered and said, "I was sent only to the lost sheep of the house of Israel." But she came and began to bow down before Him, saying, "Lord, help me!" And He answered and said, "It is not good to take the children's bread and throw it to the dogs." But she said, "Yes, Lord; but even the dogs feed on the crumbs which fall from their masters' table." Then Jesus said to her, "O woman, your faith is great; it shall be done for you as you wish." And her daughter was healed at once.—**Matthew 15:21–28**

Matthew wrote this story sometime in the mid 70s CE to Jewish Christians with deep and intense boundary problems. As Jews, familiar with their heritage and traditions, they were forced to include gentile converts to Christianity who were "foreigners," aliens, and outsiders, considered by many Jews to be "unclean."

It is not hard to understand this mentality because it is so prevalent in prison. Isn't the root of much of the hatred and violence among prisoners the belief that we belong to a group, or a race, or a religion that is "a cut above" the other group? Don't we see ourselves as the privileged ones who belong, and others as the "foreigners"? If Matthew came to speak in prison, he would tell us the story of this remarkable Canaanite woman.

In the story, Jesus actually calls the woman a "dog!" During Jesus' time, gentiles were frequently referred to as dogs by the Jews. Scavengers who ate whatever they found, dogs were considered unclean, as were those who were not members of the Jewish community. At the time, Jesus apparently believed that he was sent only to the Jews. The disciples had a simple solution: "Get rid of her" (v. 23).

Matthew tells his listeners that Jesus doesn't work like that. He listens to her and discovers she is a person in her own right, who loves her daughter so much she is willing to humiliate herself (v. 25) before the One she believes can make her daughter well again. Would we do any differently if our daughter were deeply ill? Matthew is trying to tell his Jewish readers, and us, that the "foreigner," as it turns out, is not much different from us. Jesus, himself, came to this change in attitude as he encountered her. As a result, this "foreigner" (a woman no less) changed the entire direction of his mission!

The question for us becomes: *Who is the "foreigner" in our life in prison?* Perhaps we are a "foreigner" to someone else? Perhaps our cherished beliefs and values are seen as inferior to the others' beliefs and values. The ongoing group drama in prison doesn't allow this consideration, as we seem so lost in our own self-righteousness and preoccupation with retaliation for even the slightest gesture of perceived disrespect.

Matthew is inviting us to another point of view. He is calling us to model our thoughts and actions on the example of Jesus. In God's saving plan for humanity there is no room for an "us versus them" attitude, no exclusion based on gender or race, not even on religion! When we recognize that we are no different from the "foreigner," we can find the deep kinship and true solidarity we have with one another, especially here in prison. We are all learners, fellow travelers, trying to find meaning in our lives, facing the One who brings us together, without exclusion, favoritism, or privilege.

A Contemplative View of the Lord's Passion

And they come to a piece of land called Gethsemane and Jesus says to his disciples, "Sit here while I pray." And he takes Peter, James, and John with him and he begins to go into shock and be overcome. And he says to them, "I feel so utterly sad that I could die. Stay here and keep watch." And going on a little further he collapsed onto the ground and he prays that if it were possible, the Hour might pass him by. He was saying, "ABBA, Father, all things are possible for you; take away this cup from me; yet not as I will, but as you will." And he comes and finds [the disciples] sleeping. And he says to Peter, "Simon, are you sleeping? Do you not have the strength to keep watch for a single hour? Keep watch and pray so that you may not enter into temptation. The spirit is eager, but the flesh is weak." And going away he prayed, using the same expression. And coming a second time he found them sleeping, for their eyes were very heavy. They did not know how to answer him. And he comes a third time and says to them, "You can sleep from now on and take your rest; it is all over. The Hour has come, and behold, the Human One is betrayed into the hands of the sinners. Rise. Let us go forth. Behold the one who is betraying me approaches."—**Mark 14:32–42** *(Translation by Michael Casey)*

The drama of the Lord's Passion—his betrayal, arrest, trial, conviction, tortuous death, and final vindication—starts with his encounter with his "Father." This scene has come to be known as the "Agony in the Garden," or "Gethsemane," which is the place just outside of Jerusalem where the encounter occurred.

This scene has a particular meaning for men in prison as it holds the key to true inner freedom, if only we have the eyes to see it.

The scene shows a Jesus we are not used to seeing. It shows his inner consciousness like few other scenes. For one thing, in our time, we come to think of Jesus as always possessing a confident reliance on the Ultimate Mystery that he called *Father*. Not so here, at least at first sight.

His going into "shock" and being "overcome" (v. 33) describe a person experiencing a severe trauma. We can only guess at the origins of the trauma. As children we were taught that Jesus had divine knowledge of his impending torture and death. But now, as so many of us face our own inner traumas and experiences of a lifetime, maybe we have a better clue as to his agony. It appears to be a profound disturbance in his soul.

He tells his friends, "I feel so utterly sad that I could die" (v. 34). He looks to his friends, as we would, for support. He is not testing them. He does not want to do this alone. This is the deep internal struggle of a leader coming to terms with the consequences of his revolutionary teaching. The Source of his teaching, namely his relationship with his Father, appears not to help him even now in the final hours of his life.

What does he do? Cut and run (he could have), or stand his ground? Who among us in the deep terror of our dark nights has not come upon this same dilemma? Do we face our inner demons or cut and run to the closest diversion or addiction that will once again distract us from the reality of our inner life?

Now comes the pivotal moment of the scene; this is his answer to his dilemma: "Yet not as I will but as you will"

(v. 36). For those familiar with centering prayer, this "Yet" is Jesus' sacred word. This "Yet not as I will but as you will" is Jesus' consent to the presence and action of the Father in his life. No different than the consent we give when we use our sacred word in the depths of our centering prayer experience. Jesus is saying, as we are saying, *I submit to you, because it is not about me; it is about you.*

Commentators talk about Jesus' "obedience" to the Father here. But this is no ordinary obedience, as in *I'll do what you tell me because you're in charge.* No: this obedience comes from a recognition that the Father is deserving of his trust. It is a reframing of his inner conflict in the light of his relationship with the Father. It comes from Jesus' lifelong, intimate relationship with the Father, and it is this intimate relationship we call *contemplation.* The heart of the contemplative experience, the Silence of contemplative prayer, is the recognition that God is indeed with us. God doesn't tell us in words, but the realization of his presence is just as real.

Out of Jesus' contemplative experience of the Father, his "resting" or "abiding," his true destiny is formed. In the middle of his night terror he remembers the faithfulness of his Father, even though he may not experience his closeness in the middle of his terror. Jesus' "Yet" is the turning point of the entire Passion story. It explains the near-absolute silence of Jesus in the next twenty-four hours of the drama.

Now, even before his arrest, he can say to his overwhelmed companions "it is all over." He has found his way; he can get up off the ground and support his friends to do the same (v. 42). If we can bear the internal torment, we, too, come to find our destiny in the still moments of our prayer. Through our freedom we will find our destiny, if we have the eyes to see it.

The Coming of Christ Our Brother

Now in those days a decree went out from Caesar Augustus, that a census be taken of all the inhabited earth. This was the first census taken while Quirinius was governor of Syria. And everyone was on his way to register for the census, each to his own city. Joseph also went up from Galilee, from the city of Nazareth, to Judea, to the city of David which is called Bethlehem, because he was of the house and family of David, in order to register along with Mary, who was engaged to him, and was with child. While they were there, the days were completed for her to give birth. And she gave birth to her firstborn son; and she wrapped Him in cloths, and laid Him in a manger, because there was no room for them in the inn.

In the same region there were some shepherds staying out in the fields and keeping watch over their flock by night. And an angel of the Lord suddenly stood before them, and the glory of the Lord shone around them; and they were terribly frightened. But the angel said to them, "Do not be afraid; for behold, I bring you good news of great joy which will be for all the people; for today in the city of David there has been born for you a Savior, who is Christ the Lord. This will be a sign for you: you will find a baby wrapped in cloths and lying in a manger." And suddenly there appeared with the angel a multitude of the heavenly host praising God and saying, "Glory to God in the highest, and on earth peace among men with whom He is pleased."—**Luke 2:1–14**

By now we are very familiar with the Christmas story: Mary and Joseph leave Nazareth, travel to Bethlehem, and have their child. Angels tell shepherds who themselves bear witness to this child born in a stable, laid in a feeding basket because there was no room for the family in the inn. In fact, we are so familiar with the story that, as we hear it, our minds are distracted and we drift off to the joy and sadness of past Christmases and time spent alone during the holidays. We get caught up in these memories, moving quickly away from the reality of the birth of Christ to the culture of the Christmas season. When we make this shift, we miss the dramatic reality of the Divine coming into our world, and an opportunity to accept the invitation of Christmas.

We are told simply that this child, Jesus, born of the poor, young Jewish girl, is the Son of God, Christ the Savior, the liberator of his people and liberator of us. Yet, as I said earlier, it took the Church well over three hundred years to even begin to describe in words what this reality actually means. Their formula is simply this: at his birth Jesus was "fully human and fully divine."

If he was "fully human" then, like the rest of us, he had to learn about how to live in his world, and discover who he was. Like us, if he was "fully human," he had to learn about friendship and make mistakes about his own identity. He had to learn to trust his parents, believe his rabbi, and follow his call to personal integrity. Just as we do. Most importantly for us, he had to learn about God and cope with the Divine inviting him into a deep and intimate relationship. Just as we do.

But if he was also at the same time "fully divine," as our tradition tells us, then his human maturing process was made all the more complicated. This is where the Christmas story takes on personal meaning for each of us. Jesus had to come to terms with the Divine breaking into his life in powerful ways. It makes no sense to think that the reality of the Divine in his life was easy or natural or without conflict—for this would not be "human." Like us, he must have been confused, fearful, and at times angry at the utterly mysterious notion of the powerful way the Divine was impacting the outcome of his life. Remember, this "fully human, fully divine" person did not become "king of the world." Rather, he was rejected by his religious authorities, arrested, put on trial, convicted, and executed.

If he was "like us in all things," as St. Paul says, then he was touched and taken by the suffering around him. And, judging from things he said as an adult, he was deeply annoyed at the way the religious leaders of his time laid the burden of heavy guilt on people who had sincere spiritual inclinations. And yet, because he was "fully divine" he could respond to people in the way we believe only the Divine can do. If one looks closely at Jesus' life it becomes clear that it was his trust in his relationship with God that explains so much of his identity. It was the human faith of Jesus that became the single most important factor in his life.

Recognizing the faith of Jesus in the Divine (for whom he used the most intimate word, *Father*), we arrive at the heart of the mystery of Christmas. Christmas is actually celebrating the intimate joining of the Divine and the human in the person of Jesus, the Christ. God himself in the person of Christ has become our brother. As our brother, our modest, little human life is forever intimately joined into the Divine Life Itself. Merry Christmas!

> You are as You are, and I am as I am. That which I am I offer you, Lord God. For you are it entirely.
> —*The Cloud of Unknowing*

Some members of the Prison Contemplative Fellowship

Part 4

Prisoner to Prisoner

Plain Talk for Desperate Times

The following are comments by prisoners who have experienced the depths and despair of prison life and found a way to their own freedom.

Why Do You Practice Centering Prayer?

I do centering prayer to have a relationship with the Divine. It shows me what not to pass onto my children. Slowly, a little at a time, I seem to find the real me, or my true self. It also helps me see how I became the person I became in order to survive. Centering prayer helps me find ways to break the pattern and become somebody I finally like. I'm becoming the person, not the prison number. —**Jeff Clay**

For me it's about finding the truth, stripping away the layers of pain, shame, and false identities. Digging beneath the exterior, opening wounds, tearing off the mask, confronting my innermost ambiguities. Centering prayer allows the possible to slowly manifest, while creating new thoughts, deeper understanding, feelings of hope, ambition, confidence. During my meditations I sometimes see myself as this tiny orb flashing through the heavens, cycling beyond our universe, in the attempt to become a better man.—**Shorty Cavanaugh**

I find that meditation brings me the most healthy treatment I have ever experienced. It opens doors to my "stuff" that I need to deal with, and so often avoid. To be able to tap into those things that I've stored away, not even knowing that I had them stored away, brings a sense of freedom, finally.

This experience of sitting still, this internal quietness, is beyond my ability to express. It simply must be ventured into by an open-minded participant. We are each unique and priceless. Centering prayer gives me a great sense of my relationship with God.

This practice also affords us an opportunity to move into our own inner being that is up close and personal. It gives us a real knowledge of who we really are at our core. I suggest to anyone thinking about starting a centering prayer practice: if you are truly seeking, try it for yourself.—**Angel Estelle**

With centering prayer I am gaining an awareness of how much time and effort I've spent going into hiding from myself, family, friends, society at large, and ultimately God. For me, centering prayer is not about overcoming those fears that I've spent so much time trying to hide. It's more of a "coming over": a process of reintegration at a new level. I find myself being reintroduced to elements of

my being I'd long forgotten about but never really ceased looking for. I was looking in all the wrong places.
—**Josh Gilmore**

Centering prayer has opened me to seek a personal relationship with God within me, personal and intimate. I am a person so close to this God that it gives me faith in something greater than a label.—**Kenneth Krantz**

I practice centering prayer because it offers another avenue for expanding my relationship with God. We make ourselves available to allow God to speak to us. It allows us to face issues in our lives that linger below the surface of our conscious mind. It gives me energy to refocus my life where it belongs, at the feet of the Master. This is where I find peace.
—**Thomas Sanchez**

Would You Recommend Centering Prayer to People in Prison?

I could give several reasons, but I'll give just one: it helps people become better people.—**Zane Jenkins**

There is a peace in the silence that tells you that you are OK even when you are not OK. You can still hurt and be hurt, but you have a choice about what you do with the hurt you experience. You have a choice about the desire to inflict hurt because of the hurt you experience. The time we spend with the intention to be with God becomes the

time we do spend with God; only it's on God's terms. This has added a whole new dimension to my life.
—**Lawrence Hamilton**

Through my practice I have come to know God on a very intimate level, for the first time in my life. Now I've been a believing Christian for many years, but the relationship I felt between my Father in heaven and myself has never (nor could it have ever) reached this point, without sitting in the Silence of centering prayer. I have found strength in this silence that I have searched my whole life for.—**James Dexter**

Centering prayer has allowed me to find the space I need in decision-making. It allows me to breathe, to accept things as they come, to let God provide the answers or the direction I need to travel.—**Beau Hays**

Just experiencing the difference between the Outside God and the Inside God as we do in centering prayer offers us a profound wisdom. We can begin to see that it is only our ego-consciousness that creates the illusion that God is separate, and non-intimate with us. This experience that comes from centering prayer is meant for everyone and everyone should receive it. Yes, I recommend centering prayer for anyone interested in the inner journey.—**Schacobie Manning**

Suffering is a part of prison. But that suffering need not be meaningless. A centering prayer practice can help you discover the pearl of great price within yourself. That's why the caged bird sings. He understands the redemptive value of his suffering.—**Paul Dietering**

The plant is on a perch in a high corner of Greystone Chapel in Folsom Prison

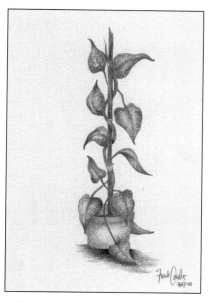

The Elephant Ear by Franky Carrillo

*This vibrant and beautiful plant is still able to grow, flourish, and bring happiness to those who take the time to gaze on it in such a dark place. This growth is occurring in a mere handful of soil, held in a tiny space—the pot—the cell—prison. I found the symbol of the plant rang true in my life. It gave me a sense of God's presence. The stick is in the center of the pot, the center of someone's life, where one can lean on, find support, and give it a firm foundation.—**Franky Carrillo***

Suggestions for Further Reading and Resources

Au, Wilkie, and Noreen Cannon Au. *God's Unconditional Love: Healing Our Shame.* Mahwah, N.J.: Paulist Press, pp. 35–58

Bourgeault, Cynthia. *Centering Prayer and Inner Awakening.* Cambridge, Mass.: Cowley Publications, 2004

Finley, James. *Merton's Palace of Nowhere: 25th Anniversary Edition.* Notre Dame, Ind.: Ave Maria Press, 2003

Keating, Thomas. *The Human Condition.* New York: Paulist Press, 1999

_____. *Intimacy with God.* New York: Crossroad Publishing, 2000

_____. *Invitation to Love: The Way of Christian Contemplation.* New York: Continuum, 2004

_____. *Open Mind, Open Heart: 20th Anniversary Edition.* New York: Continuum, 2006

May, Gerald. *Addiction and Grace.* San Francisco: Doubleday and Company, 1975

Mayers, Gregory. *Listen to the Desert: Secrets of Spiritual Maturity from the Desert Fathers and Mothers.* Liguori, Mo.: Liguori Publications, 1996

Merton, Thomas. *Contemplative Prayer*. New York: Image Books, 1996

Rohr, Richard. *Breathing Under Water: Spirituality and the Twelve Steps*. Cincinnati: Franciscan Media, 2011

_____. *Everything Belongs: The Gift of Contemplative Prayer*. New York: Crossroad Publishing, 2003

_____. *Immortal Diamond*. San Francisco: Jossey-Bass, 2013

Resources

Center for Action and Contemplation: P.O. Box 12464, Albuquerque, NM 87195-2464 cac.org

Contemplative Outreach, 10 Park Place, Second Floor Suite B., Butler, NJ 07405, www.contemplativeoutreach.org

Human Kindness Foundation, P.O. Box 61619, Durham, NC 27715, www.humankindness.org

Prison Contemplative Fellowship, P.O. Box 1086, Folsom, CA 95763-1086, USPCF.org

Acknowledgments

This book is a distillation of the work of contemporary masters of the Christian contemplative tradition. These great teachers of our time, whose writings are implicit or sometimes quoted in the book, include Thomas Keating, Richard Rohr, Thomas Merton, Cynthia Bourgeault, Gregory Mayers, William Johnson, Karl Rahner, William Dych, and Gerald May. Some of these spiritual masters have generously and personally brought their spirituality directly to the incarcerated.

Thanks as well to those members of the Prison Contemplative Fellowship who in our prayer meetings since 2009 were willing to share their point of view regarding contemplative prayer in prison. Their insights form the substance of the book.

I am also grateful to my friends and colleagues who listened to my thoughts, shared their own experiences, edited the material, and encouraged this work. They include: Scott Wood, Chuck McIntyre, Tim O'Connell, Ellie Shea, Fred O'Connor, Jim Zazzera, Jerre Sears, Janice Boyd, Susan Turpin, Ned Dolejsi, Kathy Moore, Al Franklin, Richard Spohn, and former volunteers Mike Kelley, Frank Brown, and Barbara Rodriquez.

Franky Carrillo, now a free man who spent twenty years in prison for a crime he did not commit, is responsible for the drawings in this book. Franky's great contribution to our classes on contemplative prayer led to the method of teaching abstract notions of prayer through drawings.

This work's original edition could not have gone to press without the patience and practical insight, as well as the computer skills, of Kristi Daggett. Thank you. Thank you also to Martin Rowe at Lantern Books for taking on this edition.

Finally, my wife, Cherla, was ever open to the ideas of the book, often made helpful editorial suggestions, and offered me encouragement to press on when I wondered if it was worth the effort.

About the Author

Ray Leonardini is a former lawyer who practiced government and nonprofit law for nearly thirty years. After his retirement, he turned toward his foremost area of interest: the Christian contemplative tradition. For the last nine years, as a volunteer chaplain, he has led meditation groups and taught contemplative prayer and the spiritual journey at Folsom State Prison in California. He is also the Director of the Prison Contemplative Fellowship, an association of current and former prison inmates, chaplains, and volunteers committed to reaching out to prisoners and their families on their travels along the spiritual path.

The Thomas Keating Reader
Selected Writings from the Contemplative Outreach Newsletter

The Transformation of Suffering
*Reflections on September 11
and the Wedding Feast in Cana Galilee*

BOOKS ABOUT CENTERING PRAYER

Carl J. Arico
A Taste of Silence
Centering Prayer and the Contemplative Journey

P. Gregg Blanton
Mind over Marriage
*Transforming Your Relationship Using Centering Prayer
and Neuroscience*

Peter Traben Haas
The God Who Is Here
*A Contemplative Guide to Transforming Your Relationship
with God and the Church*

Paul David Lawson
Old Wine in New Skins
Centering Prayer and Systems Theory

Murchadh Ó Madagáin
Centering Prayer and the Healing of the Unconscious

About the Publisher

LANTERN BOOKS was founded in 1999 on the principle of living with a greater depth and commitment to the preservation of the natural world. In addition to publishing books on animal advocacy, vegetarianism, religion, and environmentalism, Lantern is dedicated to printing books in the U.S. on recycled paper and saving resources in day-to-day operations. Lantern is honored to be a recipient of the highest standard in environmentally responsible publishing from the Green Press Initiative.

LANTERNBOOKS.COM